THE POWER OF PASTA

Olwen Woodier

A Garden Way Publishing Book

 Storey Communications, Inc.
Pownal, Vermont 05261

Illustrations by Liz Hemingway
Cover Photo by Charles Trottier
Book Design by Andrea Gray

Special Thanks to The Vermont Pasta Company,
Winooski, Vermont

© **Copyright by Storey Communications, Inc.**

The name Garden Way Publishing has been licensed to Storey Communications, Inc. by Garden Way, Inc.

Printed in the United States by Alpine Press
First Printing, June, 1985

Library of Congress Cataloging in Publication Data
Woodier, Olwen 1942-
    The power of pasta.

    1. Cookery (Macaroni) I. Title.
TX809.M17W66 1985   641.8'22   84-48812
ISBN 0-88266-385-2
ISBN 0-88266-384-4 (pbk.)

Contents

Preface   v

Introduction   1

Getting To Know Pasta   13

Homemade Pasta   23

Recipes Featuring Homemade Pasta   33

Baked Pasta   45

Pasta with Legumes   55

Pasta-and-Meat Entrées   65

Pasta and Seafood   77

Oriental Pasta   91

Pasta Salads   101

Pasta and Vegetables   113

Special Sauces   123

No-Cook Sauces and Dressings   135

Quantity Pasta Recipes   145

Index   150

This book is dedicated to my husband Richard Busch, to all our athlete friends who are true believers in the power of pasta, and to my favorite football team, the New York Giants. Special thanks go to Jill Mason, my editor, who painstakingly checked all my recipes for clarity.

Preface

Before I started researching pasta, I could never fathom the meaning of "Yankee Doodle went to town/Riding on a pony/Stuck a feather in his hat/And called it 'macaroni'." It had always seemed a rather whacky song until I read that during the time of the American Revolution, the word macaroni was used by young English fops to mean something fashionable and elegant. The English soldier who wrote that the feather was "macaroni" meant to convey the idea that it was exceptional. And that is exactly what these recipes are all about — they are exceptionally delicious, and most are quick and easy to prepare. Not only do they suit the purse, they also suit our busy lifestyles and our notions of good health.

INTRODUCTION

If the Italians seem passionately preoccupied with pasta, it's not surprising when you consider the hundreds of different shapes and sizes available to them in the land of their birth. It's no exaggeration to say that there are more than enough to provide a different dish of pasta every day for at least two years. Here in America, 325 dies are in existence. (Dies are the pierced metal discs used in the preparation of certain types of pasta.) However, whereas the average American eats spaghetti and meatballs or macaroni and cheese, our Italian counterparts look forward to a multitude of dishes, including tortellini, pansotti, cannelloni, fusilli, tagliatelle, linguini, and a vast number of cut shapes. Their pasta is likely to be served with seafood, ground walnuts, beans, butter and cream, ground meat, fresh vegetables, or, very simply, olive oil, garlic, and mushrooms.

At sixty pounds per person per year, the Italians lead the field in pasta consumption. The Swiss are next in line with twenty pounds per person, followed by the French, who, although not concerned with eating a wide variety, consume thirteen pounds. Those taking fourth place in this starchy competition come from the great American melting pot and weigh in at ten pounds of pasta per person per year.

Although the Orientals don't eat oodles of noodles, a number of noodle varieties are eaten in Japan, Korea, Laos, Cambodia, Thailand, Tibet, Indonesia, Vietnam, Burma, and the Philippines. Along with rice, noodles are eaten in quantity in China. In the northern provinces, where wheat is grown, noodles are eaten at the main meal. In China's southern regions, where rice is the staple crop, noodles are treated less seriously and, made from rice flour, are usually eaten as a snack.

While the exact origin of pasta is unknown, some scholars of Chinese food place the date in the sixth century B.C., during the time of Confucius. However, reliefs lining an Etruscan tomb in Cerveteri, Italy, from the fourth century B.C., depict a variety of pasta-making and pasta-cutting utensils, leaving us with no doubt that noodles were well established in Italian cooking long before Marco Polo took his trip to China in the thirteenth century. During the Middle Ages, many cultures made pasta dough and produced a number of different forms. Some were stuffed with meat or

vegetables, others were dried. It is documented by poet Horace and epicure Apicius, that the Romans took pleasure in eating leeks, chickpeas, and lasagna, and a dish of fried pasta with honey. In the fifteenth century, when pasta shops were common, Italian authorities regulated the weight and price of pasta in order to protect customers from unscrupulous merchants. It was not until the seventeenth century that pasta caught on as a homemade item. Then, it seems, all the women of Naples started to make their own. At about the same time, some genius discovered one of the best uses for tomatoes (which had been brought from South America a century earlier) and turned them into a thick, rich sauce. Thus was born the famous combination of pasta and tomato sauce.

Pasta did not reach the shores of the United States until 1786, introduced not by an Italian immigrant, but by Thomas Jefferson. Traveling in Europe as ambassador to France, Jefferson had visited Italy, and when the time came for him to return to America, he brought a spaghetti die with him. Pasta was not produced here commercially until 1848, however, and did not really take off until the Department of Agriculture introduced a hard durum wheat to this country's farming community at the beginning of the twentieth century. Today, this wheat is grown in Montana, Minnesota, California, Arizona, New Mexico, South Dakota, and North Dakota (which produces 80 percent of the wheat grown in this country).

Eating for Health

Pasta consumption in the United States has been increasing steadily during the last decade, and the increase continues at a formidable rate. Spaghetti is the favorite form and accounts for 40 percent of all pasta sales in this country. There are several reasons for pasta's popularity: It is economical, satisfying, and healthful. According to a USDA bulletin, *Nutritive Value of Foods* (1981), 1 cup cooked "spaghetti" (approximately 2 ounces uncooked) contains the following nutrients:

Protein	7–14 grams (depending on the brand and whether the pasta is "enriched")

Carbohydrates	39 grams
Calcium	14 milligrams
Phosphorus	85 milligrams
Iron	1.4 milligrams
Potassium	103 milligrams
Thiamin (B–1)	.23 milligrams
Riboflavin (B–2)	.13 milligrams
Niacin (B)	1.8 milligrams
Calories	190 if cooked al dente, 155 if cooked tender

Contrary to popular belief, pasta is not fattening. It is the accompanying sauce that converts this low-fat, low-calorie food into a dish of caloric indecency. A 4-ounce portion of dried macaroni contains about 450 calories, only 2.8 percent of vegetable fat, and, depending on the brand, anywhere from 12 to 30 grams of protein. (The fat content in 4 ounces of uncooked *egg* noodles is 9 percent, compared to the 2.8 percent found in the same weight of pasta made from flour and water.)

When made from semolina (the heart of hard durum wheat), whole wheat, soy, or Jerusalem artichoke flours, pasta falls into the category of complex carbohydrates, making it one of the most healthful foods we can eat. All carbohydrates, complex and simple, are manufactured by plants from carbon dioxide and water during the process of photosynthesis. However, it is important to make the distinction between complex and simple carbohydrates. *Complex* carbohydrates are found in such foods as pasta, whole grain breads, whole grain cereals, brown rice, potatoes (baked or boiled, preferably with the skins), beans, nuts and seeds, and fresh fruits and vegetables. These foods are low in fat, sugar, and sodium, and they supply protein, vitamins, minerals, and fiber (roughage). Foods in the category of *simple* carbohydrates (refined sugars and starches found in white bread, cakes, pies, potato chips, candy, and sodas) contain lots of calories and little or no nutrition. These are the "empty" calories that dieters try to avoid.

The advantage of eating complex carbohydrates is that you need less fat and less food to produce a feeling of satisfaction and a higher level of nutrition, both desirable aims if you're concerned with your health and weight. However, the *incomplete vegetable protein* in pasta, brown rice, whole wheat bread, whole grains, and fresh vegetables is more nutritionally beneficial when combined with

one or two of the following complementary sources of protein: beans, nuts, seeds, eggs, cheese, milk, meat, fish, or poultry. If, for instance, you were serving Pasta Primavera (pasta with fresh vegetables), you would need to add a *complementary protein* such as grated Parmesan cheese to create a protein balance.

The concept of complementary proteins is traditional in many cultures. The Chinese team noodles with tofu and vegetables, the Japanese eat soy sauce with noodles or rice, the Mexicans mix corn and beans, the Italians have their pasta and beans. Indeed, the internationally popular combination of beans and grains can also be found in Jewish, Middle Eastern, and Spanish-speaking countries. Dishes such as the Creole red beans and rice and the southern Hoppin' John (black-eyed peas, rice, and onions) provide American examples of complementary proteins.

A peek into Italian cookbooks shows that the Italians are masters at practicing this system of protein complements. Their diet, if followed in moderation, is similar to the one recommended for Americans by the Senate Select Committee on Nutrition in its 1977 report, *Dietary Goals*.

It is recommended that for optimal health and energy, between 60 and 70 percent of the average person's daily caloric intake should be in the form of complex carbohydrates. According to Dr. Bernard Gutin, Professor of Applied Physiology and Education at Columbia University, the average daily diet should include no more than 10 percent of meat protein, and he believes that 5 percent would be adequate. "For example," he says, "a healthy combination for dinner would include a small portion (2–3 ounces) of meat, poultry, or fish, eaten with high-protein grains like pasta, bulgur, or brown rice, plus a leafy vegetable or green salad. Or substitute a baked potato and a slice of whole-grain bread for the grains. In turn, the meat protein could be replaced by beans, low-fat cheese, nuts and seeds, eggs, tofu, or milk (skim, low-fat, or buttermilk)."

The Department of Agriculture's Human Nutrition Center in Washington, D.C., reports that the ideal diet for the average person would involve reducing fat consumption to 25 percent of the daily caloric intake. High-cholesterol, saturated animal fats should be cut to a minimum, with the balance provided by polyunsaturated fats.

Cholesterol is produced naturally by the body, but the consumption of saturated fats raises the natural cholesterol level of some people. Studies carried out at New York's Rockefeller University show that some of us excrete unwanted cholesterol, some of us compensate by cutting back on the production of fat, and some of us store cholesterol in the blood stream. An excessive amount of cholesterol in the blood stream leads to blockage of the coronary arteries, resulting in the heart disease, atherosclerosis, which causes heart

SOURCES OF COMPLEX CARBOHYDRATES

Fresh fruit and vegetables. Eat fruit and vegetables for snacks or to accompany any meal. Beware of avocados, for they are high in calories. However, they are also high in protein.

Grains. Buckwheat groats (kasha), bulgur, cracked wheat, millet, oats, brown rice, wild rice, and coarse cornmeal (polenta).

Whole grain cereals. Rolled oats, shredded wheat, muesli, granola (low-sugar), bran, wheat germ, and Grape Nuts.

Pasta. Pasta made from enriched semolina durum, whole wheat, soy, or Jerusalem artichoke flour or enriched with eggs, spinach, or nuts, for example.

Whole grain flours. Whole wheat, triticale, buckwheat, cornmeal, rye, rice, barley, soy, and oatmeal flours make dense breads when used alone; when combined with all-purpose flour they are hearty and still very nutritious.

Seeds and nuts. All types. Use coconut, cashew nuts, peanuts roasted in oil, and pumpkin seeds in moderation, for they are higher in saturated fats than almonds, brazil nuts, filberts, hazelnuts, pecans, walnuts, and sunflower seeds.

Dried legumes. Peas, black-eyed peas, garbanzo beans (chickpeas), black beans (turtle beans), Great Northern beans, kidney beans, pinto beans, red beans, navy beans, cannelini beans, soybeans, lima beans, and lentils.

attacks. However, "storers" are able to lower or raise their cholesterol level by controlling the ratio of unsaturated fat to saturated fat that they consume.

Saturated fats are present not only in high-fat meats, chicken fat and skin, bacon fat, lard, salt pork, suet, butter, cheese, and whole-milk products, they are also found in chocolate, coconut, palm oil, and the hydrogenated oils in some stick margarines and solid shortening. (The cautious would be better off using the soft margarines that come in tubs.) *Monosaturated* fats are found in almonds, brazil and cashew nuts, peanut products, avocados, olives, and fish and shellfish (including the much maligned lobster). Considered neutral, they neither raise nor lower blood cholesterol. However, recent observations indicate that the fatty acids in fish and shellfish oils (lower in many cases than those found in poultry) may, in fact, lower cholesterol and reduce the likelihood of clots forming in the arteries. *Polyunsaturated* fats actually help lower the blood cholesterol and are present in safflower, corn, soybean, sunflower, sesame, cottonseed, and walnut oils.

All my recipes are made with low-fat ricotta, mozzarella, or cottage cheese, and if there is any difference between these and their whole-milk counterparts, it's that they produce a lighter sauce. I also use an excellent blend of unsalted butter and margarine. The texture is creamy and the flavor almost indistinguishable from pure butter. When it comes to heavy cream though, it is difficult to substitute light cream or half-and-half in some recipes because the heavy cream is often used as a thickening agent.

When a recipe calls for ground beef, I use low-fat "round" beef and add a small quantity of sausage meat or pork for flavor. I like to cook meat sauces at least a day ahead of time. Once they've been refrigerated for several hours (or overnight), the fat can be scraped off the top.

Eating for Competition

Besides clearing up the misconception about protein as an energy food, the Senate Select Committee on Nutrition reported that the average American consumes too much protein — twice the amount needed by the

Low-Fat Dietary Comparison Chart

	PROTEIN (grams)	FAT (grams)	CHOLESTEROL (milligrams)	CALORIES
Mozzarella, part-skim, 4 ounces	32	20	72	320
Mozzarella, whole, 4 ounces	24	28	108	360
Ricotta, part-skim, 1 cup	28	19	72	340
Ricotta, whole, 1 cup	28	32	112	430
Cottage cheese, creamed, 1 cup	28	10	34	235
Cottage cheese, dry, 1 cup	25	1	16	125
Cottage cheese, low-fat, 1%, 1 cup	28	2	9	165
Parmesan, grated, ½ cup	21	15	76	225
Romano, grated, ½ cup	26	13	120	205
Yogurt, regular, 1 cup (8 ounces)	8	8.3	30	152
Yogurt, low-fat, 1 cup (8 ounces)	8	3.7	17	123
Sour cream, 1 cup	7	48	152	495
Mayonnaise, 1 cup	2.4	180	160	1580
Cream, heavy, 1 cup	5	74	316	820
Cream, light, 1 cup	6	46	158	470
Cream, half-and-half, 1 cup	7.7	28	105	315
Butter, 1 tablespoon	0	11	31	100
Butter-margarine blend, 1 tablespoon	0	11	10	100
Margarine, 1 tablespoon	0	11	0	100
Corn oil, 1 tablespoon	0	13.6	0	120
Peanut oil, 1 tablespoon	0	13.5	0	119
Olive oil, 1 tablespoon	0	13.5	0	119
Sesame oil, 1 tablespoon	0	13.5	0	120
Sausage meat, cooked, 8 ounces	16	75	96	496
Ground beef round, cooked, 8 ounces	56	24	207	429
Ground beef chuck, cooked, 8 ounces	56	48	213	640
Ground pork, cooked, 8 ounces	56	64	200	850
Chicken with skin, cooked, 2 cups	53	24.3	144	409
Chicken without skin, cooked, 2 cups	53	8	136	309
Chicken livers, cooked, 4 ounces	26	5	846	187

This data has been taken from numerous sources including the USDA bulletin *Nutritive Value of Foods* No. 72, revised edition, 1981; USDA *Agriculture Handbook* No. 8, 1964; and manufacturers' labels.

body and most of it loaded with cholesterol from saturated animal fats. Although proteins build and repair the muscles, it is now accepted that it is the carbohydrates that supply energy for the continuous and repeated muscular contractions that occur during prolonged exercise. For this reason, sports nutritionists now advise athletes to include extra complex carbohydrates in their diet when they need to be in top form for an especially active weekend of running, skiing, climbing, swimming, or any other sport that demands *continued* physical exertion.

Carbohydrates are stored in the muscles and liver in the form of glycogen — a chain of glucose molecules made up of carbon, hydrogen, and oxygen. Glycogen breaks down during vigorous exercise and releases the energy that makes the muscles contract. Once these stores are depleted, the muscles cannot perform to their best ability until the body restores its carbohydrates again. In other words, a high-protein diet just doesn't provide the energy necessary for a sustained period of intense activity.

For maximum energy, most of today's top athletes follow a high-carbohydrate diet when training for competition. This practice, taken seriously by professional and amateur athletes, works for anyone who wants to shine in a special event.

The New York Giants, aided and abetted by trainer Ronnie Barnes and nutritionist Merle Best, have been steadily changing their diets during the past two years. As football training begins, the players are counselled to cut back on animal fats in favor of low-fat plant foods and skim-milk products. Low-fat foods are easier to digest, they contain fewer calories, and they are better sources of carbohydrates. Cutting back on meat protein is not always easy for people who were nurtured on the outdated idea that if you want to be strong and healthy you should eat steak for breakfast, lunch, and dinner. However, Merle Best reports that when the players hear that pasta, rice, breads, and other foods they love are powerful replacements, they are willing to change. Dick Rossi, the New York Giants' food consultant, has passed along three of their favorite recipes for you to try. See Quantity Pasta Recipes, page 145.

To maintain energy stores for training and performance, the goal is to eat a balanced diet with more than half of the total calories coming from complex carbohydrates. The night before the game or race, athletes fill up their glycogen stores with carbohydrates. Dinner might consist of a bowl of spaghetti (minus the sausage and meatballs), a couple of slices of 100 percent whole wheat bread, and a salad. Pizza is another favorite. A low-fat, carbohydrate dessert, such as fruit, sherbet, or angel cake rounds out the meal.

In the morning, at least two hours before the event, a high-carbohydrate breakfast is in order. This could include buckwheat or whole wheat pancakes, whole wheat French toast, a peanut butter sandwich, bran or corn muffins, fruit and low-fat yogurt, a bowl of cereal with fruit, or anything else in the same category, as long as it's not loaded with sugar (that includes honey, molasses, and corn and maple syrups). Foods containing a high percentage of sugar do give a short burst of energy, but they trigger low blood sugar, dizziness, and fatigue within a few hours.

So what does all this mean to you if you're just interested in keeping fit but not competing? It means you can eat economical and healthful meals of pasta several times a week without increasing your weight (unless you drown your pasta with butter and heavy cream too often). In fact, there's every chance that you'll lose weight if you dress your pasta with low-fat sauces and eat whole grains, vegetables, and lots of fresh fruit. Such a menu will prove to be delicious and satisfying.

GETTING TO KNOW PASTA

Pasta is the generic name for the many different shapes made from flour and water, sometimes with the addition of olive oil. When eggs are added, those products are referred to as noodles. Macaroni is the generic term for both noodles and pasta, including spaghetti and macaroni. In the United States, there are 325 different dies for shaping pasta, but only 150 forms are manufactured commercially. If we include the imported varieties and the locally produced fresh and frozen pastas, it is possible to locate over 200. In Italy, over 1,000 different shapes are made.

The larger American supermarkets often carry forty or more types, including two or three varieties of imported pastas and some made from whole wheat and Jerusalem artichoke flours. Imported pasta is usually made from "100 percent durum wheat" — semolina flour, the heart of the hard durum wheat. It is more resilient than that made from all-purpose flour (a combination of soft and hard wheat flours) and is easier to cook to that perfect doneness known as "al dente" — firm to the bite. A wider variety of imported (dried) pasta can usually be found at local specialty shops and Italian delicatessens.

Most of the specialty and Italian stores in my area (fifty miles north of New York City) also keep their freezers stocked with about a dozen varieties of fresh and frozen homemade pastas. Some are stuffed with chicken, veal, and cheeses. Others are flavored with spinach, broccoli, carrot, and whole wheat. Pasta enthusiasts will find a far greater assortment of fresh and dried pasta if they live close to a major city where there are any number of stores specializing in homemade pastas.

Pasta is used as the base for an almost infinite variety of sauces and salads and for adding texture and nourishment to soups. According to traditional Italian cooks, the long, thin shapes are more appropriate for light sauces, while the cut, hollow macaronies are suitable for chunky meat sauces and for baking. The recipes in this book suggest the use of a particular pasta, in most cases based on my personal preference; however, as you will see from the list on page 17, there are many possible substitutes.

Oriental noodles come in a variety of shapes and flavors. I have always been intimidated by recipes for Chinese noodle dough and have taken the easy way out by visiting one of my

local Oriental food stores for packets of dried noodles, or the supermarket for won ton skins. See page 18 for a list of some common Oriental noodles.

Cooking Perfect Pasta

When boiling any kind of pasta, you need 4–6 quarts of water to every pound (enough for four people). Use a pot large enough to accommodate the pasta with room to spare — for 6 quarts of water, use at least an 8-quart pot. This prevents the pasta from sticking together and helps it to cook faster. The addition of 1 teaspoon of oil will also keep the strands from sticking.

Bring the water to a rolling boil over high heat (add 1 tablespoon of salt, if desired) and add the pasta all at once. Long strands will need to be pushed into the water until completely submerged. Using a wooden fork, stir gently to separate the strands or shapes. When the water returns to a rolling boil, lower the heat to medium so that it continues to bubble without boiling over.

The pasta is done when it is tender but firm. The Italians call this "al dente" — firm to the bite. Cooking time varies according to the pasta — thick or thin, small or large, dried or fresh. If it's homemade (fresh or dried), it may take as little as 2 minutes. The cooking time for fresh pasta depends on the flour used, whether or not the dough contains eggs, and whether it is stuffed or not. As a rule, start testing long, flat pasta after 1 minute. Stuffed pastas may take anywhere from 5 to 15 minutes. When commercial dried pasta is used, follow the directions on the package, but

HOW MUCH TO COOK

- 2 ounces of dry, macaroni-type pasta yields about 1¼ cups cooked
- 8 ounces or 2 cups of dry macaroni-type pasta yields 4½–5 cups cooked
- 8 ounces of dry egg noodles yields 4 cups cooked
- 4 ounces or 1 3½-inch bundle of dry spaghetti-type pasta yields 2–2½ cups cooked
- 8 ounces or 1 4½-inch bundle of dry spaghetti-type pasta yields 4–5 cups cooked
- 12 ounces or 1 5½-inch bundle of dry spaghetti-type pasta yields 6½–7 cups cooked

Types of Italian Macaroni

PASTA	DESCRIPTION/SUBSTITUTES
Spaghetti	Long, thin, solid pasta. Substitute spaghettini, capellini, vermicelli, perciatelle, linguini, fusilli (curled), angel hair.
Macaroni	Short, cylindrical, hollow tubes. Substitute ziti, penne, elbows, mezzani, mezzanelli, bucatini, ditali, zitoni.
Flat egg noodles	Tagliatelle, tagliarini, fettuccine, fettuccelle.
Pasta for stuffing	Lasagna noodles, large tubes (manicotti, tufoli, mafalde, cannelle, grooved rigatoni).
Specialty shapes	Bows (farfalle, farfallette, farfalloni), shells (maruzze, maruzzelle, conchiglie, conchigliette), cavatelli.
Stuffed pasta	Tortelli, tortellini, ravioli, ravioletti, raviolini, agnolotti, anolini, cappelletti, pansotti.
Pasta for soups, side dishes, and children's meals	Acini di pepe, anelli, anellini, ditalini, tubetti, tubettini, stelle (stars), rotini (tiny wheels), rotelle (wheels), semi di melone (melon seeds), pasta grattingiate (grated fresh pasta), orzo ("barley"), spacemen and astronauts, capelli d'angelo (angel hair), and many, many more.

choose the shorter time listed and start testing (by tasting) several minutes before the end. This way, you'll be assured of getting perfectly cooked al dente pasta.

Drain the cooked pasta in a colander and serve immediately, or spread cannelloni, manicotti, and lasagna pieces on a clean tea towel and blot dry before continuing with a stuffed recipe. Long pasta is easier to handle if metal spaghetti tongs or a wooden "spoon" with short dowels in one side is used to transfer it from the colander to a serving dish.

Types of Oriental Noodles

CHINESE NOODLES	DESCRIPTION
Egg wheat noodles	Sold fresh or dried. Called tan mein, these noodles are yellow and range from vermicelli-thin to quarter-inch ribbon width. Eat stir fried, pan fried, boiled, or in soups. Substitute with Italian egg noodles.
Mung bean noodles	Sold dried to be soaked before cooking. They are thin and become transparent and gelatinous when cooked. Most commonly called cellophane noodles, glass noodles, bean thread noodles, fan si noodles. Use in soups, cold salads, and for deep frying.
Rice flour noodles	Sold fresh or dried. If dried, they must be soaked before cooking. These are the thin, wavy noodles, although when fresh they are usually flat, quarter-inch ribbons. Called lai fen, chow fun, mi-fun, rice sticks, and rice vermicelli. Use in soups, cold salads, and for deep frying and stir frying.
Seaweed noodles	Sold dried to be soaked before cooking. These dong yong chow noodles are best in soups and broths.

JAPANESE NOODLES	DESCRIPTION
Yam flour noodles	Sold dried under the names harusame and cellophane noodles, these are usually used in soups and broths.
Wheat flour noodles	Sold dried, these noodles range in size from vermicelli-thin to linguini-thick and are called somen, udon, and hiyamugi. Use for soups, lightly stir-fried dishes, and cold salads.
Buckwheat noodles	These are thin soba noodles and are sold dried. They can be stir fried or used in soups and cold salads.

Pasta that is to go into a baked casserole should be cooked for only two-thirds of the recommended time, because it will get softer as it finishes cooking in the oven. The exception to this rule is the thick commercial lasagna noodles. If they are not fully cooked before assembling, the baked lasagna has a tendency to come apart, and the noodles have a rubbery texture.

Serving and Eating Pasta

It is said that Ferdinand II, king of Naples in the seventeenth century, loved to dine on pasta and served it frequently to his guests. There was one major problem. The three-tined fork then in use in Italy would not hold the long strands of pasta. The king and his guests had to use their fingers. Eventually, Ferdinand's chamberlain, Gennaro Spadaccini, invented the four-tined fork to make possible the twirling of the pasta. Twirling is the accepted way to eat pasta, and Italians consider it gauche to twirl the spaghetti and the fork into a spoon. The easiest way is to slip the tines of your fork under *two or three strands* of pasta and, holding the fork upright against the edge of the bowl or plate, turn it until the pasta is wrapped around the tines. This way you'll have a few strands neatly coiled around the tines instead of the whole plateful.

Pasta is best served in warm bowls — especially when the sauce is one that doesn't have to be cooked. The warmth of the bowl helps the pasta to hold its heat longer. Most sauces are enhanced by a generous sprinkling of freshly milled black pepper and grated Parmesan or Romano cheese. Pass a pepper mill and a bowl or shaker jar of cheese at the table for the pleasure of your family and guests.

Wine is another traditional companion of pasta. When I was living in France and Switzerland during the 1960s, I was exposed to wonderful wines, including a wide selection of Italian wines, which have remained some of my favorites. However, to put together a list of Italian wines for this book, I conferred with John Martelli, Jr., co-owner and sommelier at the Mona Trattoria restaurant in Croton Falls, New York. You will find our recommendations on page 20.

A Selection of Italian Wines

WHITE WINES	COMPLEMENTARY PASTA DISHES
Corvo — dry, mellow, and full bodied	Cheese-stuffed pastas with light, creamy sauces.
Frascati — dry, smooth, and very light	Cold pasta salads with vinaigrette; seafood salads.
Orvieto — dry, slightly perfumed, and smooth	Ideal for rich cream sauces such as Alfredo.
Pinot-Grigio — dry, fruity, and full bodied	Butter sauces tossed with Parmesan cheese; cheese-stuffed pastas; chicken; veal; seafood.
Soave — dry, smooth, and medium bodied	Cold pasta salads and seafood salads in creamy dressings; butter sauces.
Verdicchio (dei Castelli di Jesi) — dry and fruity	Superb with white seafood sauces; cheese-stuffed pastas with light, creamy sauces; chicken; veal.
Vernaccia (di San Gimignano) — dry and light	Veal and chicken dishes.

RED WINES	COMPLEMENTARY PASTA DISHES
Barbaresco — dry, robust, full bodied, and smooth	Meat-stuffed pastas; meat sauces; tomato sauces.
Barbera — dry, fruity, and full bodied	Meat-stuffed pastas; meat sauces; tomato sauces.
Bardolino — dry and light	Cheese-stuffed pastas; creamy sauces; vegetable sauces; chicken; veal.
Barolo — dry, robust, full bodied, and smooth	Meat-stuffed pastas; meat, tomato, and nut sauces.
Chianti — dry, fruity, and full bodied	Tomato-based sauces; pasta stuffed with meat.
Corvo — dry, full bodied, and sometimes mellow	Meat-stuffed pastas; cheese-stuffed pastas with meat sauces; tomato, cheese, and nut sauces.
Dolcetto — dry and light	See Bardolino.
Gattinara — dry, fruity, full bodied, and smooth	Meat sauces; chicken livers; meat-stuffed pastas.
Inferno — dry and full bodied	See Corvo.
Spanna — dry, fruity, and full bodied	Red-meat-stuffed pastas; meat, tomato, and nut sauces.
Valpolicella — semi-dry, smooth, and full bodied	Red-meat-stuffed pastas; meat sauces.

Making Your Own Pasta

I first started making my own pasta ten years ago, and at one time it was eaten regularly in this household. I went through many experimentations until I was making excellent pasta, including carrot, beet, tomato, spinach, and egg noodles. I have made pasta with semolina durum flour and with all-purpose flour. Both make good pasta, but because I have to go out of my way to buy semolina durum flour, I usually make do with all-purpose. Homemade pasta is delicately tender and makes superior ravioli, cannelloni, manicotti, and lasagna because the dough can be rolled paper thin.

One advantage of making your own pasta is that you can make any number of variations that would be impossible to purchase at even the most sophisticated gourmet store. There's no point in pacing the pavement of your town or city for shrimp, walnut, or sweet red-bell-pepper pasta — you won't find those anywhere except in the enclaves of your own kitchen.

Kneading and rolling pasta dough without the aid of a pasta machine can seem like a daunting task to even the most dedicated. However, during the past decade pasta-making has proliferated in the home, thanks to the availability of these machines.

Pasta Machines

Although there are several different makes on the market, there are only two basic types: manual (hand-cranked) and electric. With a manual machine, the cook must mix the dough and knead it for about 5 minutes before feeding it through the machine rollers, which will knead the dough further. Once the dough is properly pliable, the rollers are adjusted to progressively smaller numbers so that the sheets of dough are gradually made thinner. When the dough reaches the desired thickness, it is fed between cutting blades that cut it into wide or thin noodles. A ravioli attachment is also available for these machines.

An electric machine allows you to feed the separate ingredients into the machine, which then mixes, kneads, and extrudes the dough

through a perforated die in the desired thickness and shape. Some of the electric machines can also grind, purée, and grate. However, the speed with which they knead the dough does not allow the gluten to develop a desirable elasticity; the dough may be somewhat rubbery. So when using an electric pasta machine, the results will be more acceptable if the dough is mixed and kneaded by hand or in a food processor first, as with a manual machine. The cost of a manual machine is in the neighborhood of $40; electric machines cost $200 and up.

Storing Homemade Pasta

Pasta is simply raw dough — flour and water and sometimes egg. If it is not going to be cooked right away, it can be kept refrigerated (for up to a week), frozen (for two or three months), or dried (for about two weeks).

Noodles that pass through machine cutters usually fall naturally into a nest-like shape and can be left that way or unravelled carefully and wrapped loosely around the fingers, as when starting off a ball of wool or string. Noodles that have been hand-rolled in a jellyroll shape should be separated and rolled more loosely so they can dry.

Fresh pasta that is going into the freezer need not dry completely. Seal it in freezer bags and, when needed, drop it directly into the boiling water.

If you want to dry your pasta for storage, it is possible to dry strands of pasta over broom handles, ladder-back chairs, and any number of commercial wooden drying devices; however, professionals agree that the wire-screen-tray method is superior. These trays can be stacked on top of each other, permitting the free passage of air between.

HOMEMADE PASTA

The variations in basic pasta recipes are quite mind boggling. From talking to a great number of pasta makers, I learned that noodles made with eggs and all-purpose flour are the most popular, but even so, the proportions differed from one person to the next. I have included in this chapter recipes and variations that I found easy to make. Whether I mix and knead by hand or in a food processor, I then pass the dough through a manual pasta machine to further knead the dough to the desired thickness and to cut it into wide or thin noodles. Although I roll the Cheese, Nut, and Shrimp Pastas (pages 28-30) with a manual pasta maker, I prefer to cut them into noodles by hand.

BASIC PASTA RECIPE

PREPARATION TIME: 25 MINUTES   REST TIME: 30 MINUTES   YIELD: 1 POUND

2¼ cups all-purpose flour
3 large eggs

There are many ways to vary the basic pasta dough. You can use different flours or add vegetables, herbs, ground nuts, Parmesan cheese — even ground fish or caviar. I have included several variations to get you started.

1. Mound the flour on a smooth working surface or in a very large bowl and make a well in the center.
2. Beat the eggs together and pour them into the center of the flour (adding ½ teaspoon salt, if desired). Using a fork or your hands, combine the mixture until blended and a ball forms.
3. Continue kneading until the dough is smooth and supple — about 5 more minutes. (If the dough feels too sticky, sprinkle it with 1 table-spoon flour and knead the flour into the ball. If the dough feels too hard, add *1 drop at a time* of beaten egg or vegetable oil.)
4. Place the dough in plastic wrap that has been lightly greased with vegetable oil, and let it rest for at least 30 minutes before rolling it out.

(continued on page 26)

Mixing in a Food Processor

1. Place the flour in the food processor bowl and, with the motor running, add the eggs one at a time.

2. Process until the mixture forms a ball.

3. If the dough seems too sticky, add 1 tablespoon flour and process for 10 seconds until incorporated. Then process for 40–60 seconds longer.

4. Remove the dough and wrap it in greased plastic wrap. Allow the dough to rest for at least 15 minutes before rolling it out.

Rolling by Hand

1. To make the dough more manageable, divide it into four pieces and place them on a lightly floured surface.

2. Roll each piece into a rectangle. The dough should be ⅛ inch thick for noodles or 1⁄16 inch thick for ravioli, cannelloni, tortellini, lasagna, manicotti, and any other "stuffed" recipe. (If you lay the rectangle on a clean tea towel and you can see the design of the towel through the dough, the dough is approximately 1⁄16 inch thick.)

3. *To make noodles*, roll the rectangle lengthwise like a jellyroll and slice off ⅛-, ¼-, or ½-inch widths for noodles, or 2–4-inch widths for lasagna.

To make cannelloni or manicotti, cut the rectangle into 4-inch squares and drop them into a large pot of boiling water. When the squares come to the top, remove them immediately and place them on a clean towel. When the excess moisture has been removed, lay out the squares on a tablecloth and fold the cloth so that it comes between all the squares. They must not be touching. If the pasta is not going to be used during the next hour, place the folded tablecloth in a plastic bag and refrigerate the pasta for up to two days.

To make ravioli or tortellini, cut the rectangle into 1½–2-inch squares, fill each square with a prepared stuffing, and place them in a single layer on a lightly oiled or floured tray. Refrigerate until ready to use, or freeze. When they are frozen, pack them into plastic bags and seal. Cook in the frozen state.

Rolling by Machine

1. Cut the rested dough into four pieces; flatten and lightly flour each piece as required. Keep all but one piece wrapped in the plastic to prevent them from drying out.

2. Set the pasta machine at the widest setting and run a piece of the flattened dough through the machine. Repeat at this width four times, folding it in half each time.

3. The dough will now be thoroughly kneaded, and the rollers can be set closer together for each successive rolling to obtain the desired thickness.

4. Once the pasta has reached the desired thickness, allow the sheet to stiffen somewhat (without drying out) before running it through the cutter.

Ingredient Variations

- Substitute semolina durum wheat flour for the whole amount of all-purpose flour and use 4 eggs.
- Use only 2 eggs and add ½ cup of puréed vegetables, such as spinach, broccoli, beets, carrots, or red or yellow bell peppers. Combine the vegetables with the eggs before adding them to the flour.
- Substitute whole wheat, buckwheat, triticale, rye, or semolina flour for 1 cup of the all-purpose flour and add ½ cup of puréed vegetables.
- Omit the eggs and add ½ cup of puréed vegetables.
- Add ¼–½ cup of chopped or processed fresh herbs such as parsley, basil, lemon thyme, or tarragon (a strong flavor — try 2–4 tablespoons the first time). If using dried herbs, add only 2–3 tablespoons.
- Add 1 teaspoon of curry, turmeric, or paprika for flavor and color. Nutmeg can be interesting with some cheese sauces, but it must be used judiciously — ¼ teaspoon goes a long way.

EGGLESS PASTA

PREPARATION TIME: 25 MINUTES   REST TIME: 30 MINUTES   YIELD: 1 POUND

2 cups all-purpose flour
2 tablespoons vegetable or olive oil
⅓–½ cup water with ½ teaspoon turmeric
added for color, or ⅓–½ cup beet juice

1. Mound the flour on a smooth working surface or in a very large bowl and make a well in the center.
2. Pour the oil and the water into the center of the flour and blend until a ball forms.
3. Follow the directions for Basic Pasta Recipe, page 25, beginning with step #3.

CHEESE PASTA

PREPARATION TIME: 25 MINUTES   REST TIME: 30 MINUTES   YIELD: 1 POUND

2 cups all-purpose flour
½ cup finely grated Parmesan cheese
3 large eggs

I prefer the dry imported Parmesan cheese over the moister supermarket product. If the dough seems too dry, add an extra egg, drop by drop, until it reaches the appropriate consistency.

1. Combine the flour and grated Parmesan in a blender or food processor.
2. Add the eggs, one at a time, and mix until the dough forms a ball.
3. Follow the directions for Basic Pasta Recipe, page 25, beginning with step #3.

PASTA VERDE

PREPARATION TIME: 20 MINUTES   REST TIME: 30 MINUTES   YIELD: 2 POUNDS

**10 ounces cooked spinach, drained and squeezed
  to remove moisture**
2 large eggs, beaten
4 cups flour
1 teaspoon olive oil

1. Finely chop the spinach and beat together with the eggs.
2. Place the flour on a board, make a well in the center, and add the spinach-egg mixture. Using a pastry cutter, combine the two.
3. Knead the dough for approximately 5–10 minutes and form into a ball.
4. Spread 1 teaspoon olive oil over the dough and cover with plastic wrap. Allow to rest for 20–30 minutes.
5. Roll out according to the instructions on page 26.

NUT PASTA

PREPARATION TIME: 30 MINUTES   REST TIME: 30 MINUTES   YIELD: 1 POUND

2 cups all-purpose flour
½ cup finely ground walnuts, pecans, or almonds
3–4 large eggs

1. Combine the flour and ground nuts in a blender or food processor.
2. Add the eggs, one at a time, and mix until the dough forms a ball.
3. Follow the directions for Basic Pasta Recipe, page 25, beginning with step #3.

SHRIMP PASTA

PREPARATION TIME: 30 MINUTES   REST TIME: 30 MINUTES   YIELD: 1 POUND

12 medium-size shrimp, shelled and cleaned
2½ cups all-purpose flour
2 small eggs

For a double whammy, serve this pasta with Shrimp Sauce, page 127.

1. Drop the prepared shrimp into boiling water and cook for 50 seconds or until they turn pink. Remove and rinse in cold water.
2. Purée the shrimp in a blender or food processor.
3. Combine the shrimp and flour and mix thoroughly.
4. Add the eggs, one at a time, and mix until the dough forms a ball.
5. Continue by following the directions for Basic Pasta Recipe, page 25, beginning with step #3.

PASTA ALL'UOVO

4 cups flour
5 large eggs, beaten
1 teaspoon olive oil

This recipe and the Pasta Verde recipe (page 29) are from my favorite Northern Italian restaurant in this part of the world, the Mona Trattoria, in Croton Falls, New York. See Recipes Featuring Homemade Pasta (page 33) for Mona Trattoria entrées that feature these pastas.

1. Place the flour on a board and make a well in the middle. Add the eggs and slowly incorporate with a pastry cutter.
2. Knead the dough for 5–10 minutes and form into a ball.
3. Spread 1 teaspoon olive oil over the dough and cover with plastic wrap. Allow to rest for 20–30 minutes.
4. Roll out according to the instructions on page 26.

CAROL HARCARIK'S PASTA DOUGH

PREPARATION TIME: 25 MINUTES   REST TIME: 30 MINUTES   YIELD: 1 POUND

2½ cups all-purpose flour
3 large eggs
¾ teaspoon salt
1 tablespoon olive oil
1 tablespoon lukewarm water

My neighbor Carol Harcarik makes pasta just about every Sunday. She finds this recipe to be the best she's tried so far.

1. Mound the flour on a smooth working surface or in a very large bowl and make a well in the center.
2. Beat the eggs and add to them the salt, olive oil, and water. Pour this mixture into the center of the flour. Blend until a ball forms.
3. Follow the directions for Basic Pasta Recipe, page 25, beginning with step #3.

RECIPES FEATURING HOMEMADE PASTA

My favorite Northern Italian restaurant is the Mona Trattoria of Croton Falls, New York. In that dining room, I can take my fill of the very best Italian food. The pasta is made fresh daily, and I have yet to be disappointed. Not only that, but Marisa Conti (proprietor Mona Martelli's daughter) makes enough dough so that some of her customers can come in and buy it.

Marisa works with chef Tom Elia, who makes all the stuffings and sauces (and the rest of the menu). I'm happy to say that when I asked Tom (who has been the chef at Mona's restaurant for twelve years) to let me have a couple of my favorite recipes for this book, he willingly complied. You will find them in this chapter.

The stuffed pasta dishes can be made in stages — the stuffing one day, the pasta the next, and the assembling can even wait another day. Then, either freeze them for future use or cook, eat, and enjoy them the same day.

MONA TRATTORIA'S TAGLIATELLE VERDE AL PROSCIUTTO

COOKING TIME: 10 MINUTES   YIELD: 4–6 SERVINGS

½ Pasta Verde recipe (page 29), rolled and cut
   into ¼-inch-wide noodles
½ stick (4 tablespoons) unsalted butter
2 slices prosciutto about ⅛ inch thick, cut
   in small cubes
3 cups tomato sauce
½ teaspoon freshly ground black pepper
1 tablespoon grated Parmesan cheese

1. Cook the homemade noodles in 6 quarts of boiling water for about 2 minutes.
2. While the homemade green noodles are cooking, melt the butter in a skillet and sauté the prosciutto cubes for 2–3 minutes.
3. Add the tomato sauce and cook it down for 5 minutes over medium heat. Serve over the hot tagliatelle with freshly ground black pepper and grated Parmesan cheese.

PLANNING IMPROMPTU MEALS

You can plan ahead for unexpected guests by making batches of sauce that freeze well and by stocking your cupboard with a variety of packaged pasta products and canned goods. Here's a list that may save the day:

- Boxes of several sizes and shapes of pasta.
- Cans of tomato products: purée, sauce, and whole plum tomatoes.
- Large bottle or can of olive oil.
- Cans of beans: chickpeas (garbanzo beans), red kidney beans, cannelini (white kidney beans), pinto beans, etc.
- Cans of tuna packed in water.
- Mozzarella, cubed, sliced, or grated and kept in the refrigerator or freezer.
- Romano and Parmesan cheeses, grated or left whole and kept in the refrigerator or freezer.
- A bag of walnuts, kept in the freezer.

MONA TRATTORIA'S TORTELLINI WITH CREAM SAUCE

PREPARATION TIME: 1½–2 HOURS   DRYING TIME: ½–1 HOUR   COOKING TIME: 10 MINUTES
YIELD: 8–10 SERVINGS (180 TORTELLINI)

8 ounces mortadella
4 ounces prosciutto
4 ounces raw pork
6 ounces raw chicken
1 egg yolk
¼ teaspoon freshly ground nutmeg
½ teaspoon salt
½ cup grated Parmesan cheese
⅔ **Pasta all'Uovo recipe (page 31)**

When chef Tom Elia makes filling for tortellini or cannelloni (see page 38), he has a full house in mind — the Mona Trattoria is usually jammed to capacity. Twisting 180 pieces of dough to make tortellini is a time consuming job, and you may want to divide the filling and the dough in half and freeze one half for later use.

1. Grind together the mortadella, prosciutto, pork, and chicken in a blender, food processor, or meat grinder.
2. Add the egg yolk, nutmeg, salt, and Parmesan cheese and combine thoroughly. Refrigerate while preparing the tortellini squares.
3. Roll out the dough to a ⅛–1/16-inch thickness and cut into 1½-inch squares. Cover with a damp cloth to prevent them from drying.
4. Place a small amount (about ½ teaspoon) of the filling in the center of each square. Fold the dough to make a triangle and seal the edges. Take two corners of the triangle and pinch them together. Let the stuffed tortellini air-dry for ½–1 hour.
5. If you're not going to use the pasta right away,

THE POWER OF PASTA

spread them on a cookie sheet to freeze. When frozen, seal in plastic bags for later use.

6. When you're ready to make the sauce, drop the fresh or frozen tortellini into boiling water (with 1 tablespoon oil) without crowding, and stir gently to prevent them from sticking to the bottom. When they rise to the surface, boil gently for 5 minutes or so. (If substituting commercial frozen tortellini, cook them for 10–15 minutes.) The best way to tell when they're done is to make a taste test. Don't over-cook homemade tortellini or they'll fall apart.

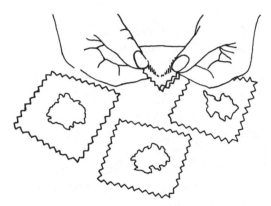

Fold the dough to make a triangle and seal the edges.

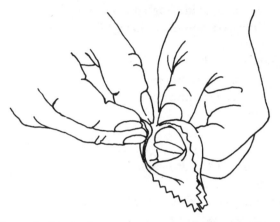

Then pinch together two corners of the triangle.

PARMESAN CREAM SAUCE

1 stick (½ cup) unsalted butter
2 cups heavy cream
½–1 cup grated Parmesan cheese

1. Melt the butter in a 2-quart saucepan.
2. Add the heavy cream and bring gently to a boil, about 2 minutes.
3. Stir in the grated Parmesan. Remove from the heat and serve over the hot tortellini.

MONA TRATTORIA'S CANNELLONI

PREPARATION TIME: 2 HOURS   CHILLING TIME: 1 HOUR   BAKING TIME: 10 MINUTES
YIELD: 15–20 SERVINGS (40 CANNELLONI)

1 large carrot, scrubbed or peeled and cut
    in 1-inch pieces
2 celery ribs, cut in 1-inch pieces
1 medium-size onion, cut in eighths
1 garlic clove
¼ pound prosciutto
1½ sticks unsalted butter
3 pounds lean ground pork
¼ cup marsala
¼ cup sherry
2 cups tomato sauce
3 tablespoons tomato paste
1 tablespoon salt
1 teaspoon coarsely ground black pepper
1 large egg, beaten
½ cup grated Parmesan cheese
1 Pasta all'Uovo recipe (page 31)
2 cups heavy cream
1 cup tomato sauce

You will probably have some pasta dough left over after you make 40 cannelloni. You can either freeze the extra dough or use it to make noodles.

1. Grind together the carrot, celery, onion, garlic, and prosciutto in a blender, food processor, or meat grinder.
2. Melt the butter in a large heavy skillet over medium heat. Add the ground vegetable mixture and sauté for 5 minutes.
3. Add the ground pork and brown for 10 minutes, turning frequently.
4. Pour in the marsala and sherry, stir to combine, and cook until liquid is evaporated — about 10 minutes.
5. Blend the 2 cups tomato sauce and the tomato paste and add to the skillet. Season with the salt and pepper and cook for 20 minutes, or until most of the liquid has evaporated.
6. Drain the filling in a fine sieve for about 5 minutes. (Reserve the juices for making soup.)
7. When the filling is cool, add the egg and Parmesan cheese and mix. Spread the filling about ¾ inch thick in two or three large rec-

THE POWER OF PASTA

tangular pans. Refrigerate for 1 hour to set and cool completely.

8. Roll out the dough to a ⅛-inch thickness. Cut into pieces 4 inches by 4 inches.

9. Slice the cooled filling into about 40 rectangular pieces 1 inch by 3½ inches.

10. Cook the squares of dough, a few at a time, in boiling water. As soon as they float to the top, remove them and rinse in cold water. (If you're making the pasta in advance, place them on a tablecloth, blot them dry, and roll them up in the cloth. Refrigerate and peel off as needed.)

11. Preheat the oven to 450° F. Place a piece of the filling at one edge of each square and roll the square like a jellyroll. (If you want to freeze them for another time, place the cannelloni on a greased cookie sheet to freeze. When frozen, place in a freezer container.)

12. Arrange the cannelloni seam-side down in two baking dishes, each containing ½ cup of the heavy cream. Pour another ½ cup of the cream over the cannelloni in each dish and drizzle ½ cup of tomato sauce over each.

13. Bake for about 10 minutes — until the cream bubbles around the edges and the cannelloni are a little browned. If the cannelloni are frozen, bake for 20 minutes, covering with foil if the pasta starts to brown too much (check after about 10 minutes).

MONA TRATTORIA'S GNOCCHI DI RICOTTA

PREPARATION TIME: 30 MINUTES   COOKING TIME: 30 MINUTES   YIELD: 8–10 SERVINGS

3½ cups all-purpose flour

3 pounds ricotta (drain through cheesecloth
  if too moist)

2 egg yolks

1 cup grated Parmesan cheese

½ teaspoon salt

½ teaspoon coarsely ground black pepper

½ teaspoon freshly grated nutmeg

1 stick (½ cup) unsalted butter

3 cups tomato sauce

½ cup heavy cream

Chef Tom Elia of Mona Trattoria's expects to use this amount of gnocchi in one day. For such a large quantity, you may prefer to freeze half of the prepared uncooked gnocchi. Spread gnocchi on a lightly floured tray to freeze. When frozen, package in plastic bags. Cook from a frozen state, following the directions for fresh gnocchi.

1. Place the flour in a large mixing bowl and make a well in the middle.
2. Put the ricotta in the middle and then add the egg yolks, Parmesan, salt, pepper, and nutmeg.
3. Stir together, adding a little more flour if the mixture feels too sticky.
4. Form the dough into a loaf. Refrigerate to firm it up, if necessary, for up to half an hour.
5. Place the dough on a floured board and cut it into eight sections. Roll each section into a cigar-shaped cylinder and cut the cylinders into ¾-inch pieces.
6. Using the back of a fork, make a slight indentation in the middle of each piece, and place each gnocchi on a floured tray or board. (Refrigerate or freeze until needed.)

7. Melt the butter in a saucepan. Add the tomato sauce and cook gently for 10 minutes.
8. Preheat the oven to 400° F. and grease a large baking dish.
9. Drop the gnocchi into a large pot of boiling water to cook. As soon as they rise to the surface, scoop them out of the water with a slot-

ted spoon and place them in the greased baking dish.
10. Add the heavy cream to the tomato sauce and bring to a quick boil. Remove from the heat.
11. Cover the gnocchi with the sauce and bake for 15 minutes. Serve.

WHITE MEAT RAVIOLI

PREPARATION TIME: 1 HOUR   COOKING TIME: 15 MINUTES   YIELD: 4–6 SERVINGS (ABOUT 40 RAVIOLI)

¾ pound ground chicken breast, veal, or drained, mashed canned tuna
2 tablespoons finely chopped shallot
2 canned plum tomatoes, drained and chopped
1 teaspoon dried leaf sage, crumbled
¼ teaspoon mace
¼ cup grated Parmesan or Romano cheese
½ cup chopped parsley
½ teaspoon coarsely ground black pepper
1 tablespoon brandy or dry sherry
1 Basic Pasta Recipe (page 25)

1. Place all the ingredients, except the pasta, in a large mixing bowl and combine thoroughly.
2. Follow the instructions for Spinach and Cheese Ravioli on page 42.
3. Serve with Red Bell Pepper Sauce (page 129) or Mushroom-and-Walnut Tomato Sauce (page 127).

SPINACH AND CHEESE RAVIOLI

PREPARATION TIME: 1 HOUR   DRYING TIME: 1 HOUR   COOKING TIME: 10 MINUTES
YIELD: 4–6 SERVINGS (ABOUT 40 RAVIOLI)

1 cup cooked chopped spinach (1 10-ounce package frozen)
1 cup part-skim ricotta cheese
⅓ cup grated Parmesan cheese
⅓ cup grated Romano cheese
¼ teaspoon ground or grated nutmeg
2 teaspoons dried basil
¼ teaspoon coarsely ground black pepper
1 garlic clove, crushed or minced
1 Basic Pasta Recipe (page 25)
4 tablespoons butter
½ cup grated Parmesan cheese

1. In a blender, food processor, or mixing bowl, combine the first eight ingredients.
2. On a lightly floured surface, roll out the pasta dough to a thickness of ⅛ inch and then cut it into 2-inch strips.
3. Place 1 teaspoon of the filling at 2-inch intervals, leaving ½ inch of space between the mounds of filling. Moisten the dough with water around the mounds and cover with a second strip of dough.
4. Press the dough firmly together around each mound of filling and cut the strip into 2-inch squares. Repeat until all the filling has been used. Allow the ravioli to dry for about 1 hour. (If you are using ravioli trays, flour the tray and cut the rolled dough so that it overlaps the edges of the tray. Press the dough gently into the molds and fill each space with 1 teaspoon of filling. Cut a second piece of dough to cover the tray and, using a rolling pin, roll over the top to seal and cut into ravioli. Dry for 1 hour.)
5. Bring water to boil in a very large pot — at least

a 6-quart size. Drop in the ravioli, about 10 at a time so as not to overcrowd, and cook for about 5 minutes.

6. Remove the ravioli from the water with a slotted spoon and place in a warm serving dish.

Toss each batch with 1 tablespoon of butter and 2 tablespoons of grated Parmesan. Keep warm.

7. Serve with a walnut sauce (page 134), a tomato sauce (page 125), Parmesan Cream Sauce (page 37), or any sauce desired.

ANN KOJIS'S SPAETZLE

PREPARATION TIME: 10 MINUTES   COOKING TIME: 10 MINUTES   YIELD: 2–3 SERVINGS

1 cup all-purpose flour
¼ cup grated Parmesan cheese
⅛ teaspoon freshly ground black pepper
1 large egg, beaten
⅓ cup milk
2 tablespoons butter

Ann Kojis is a friend and a fine cook. Spaetzle are tiny dumplings and can be added to stews and soups.

1. Mix all the ingredients, except the butter, in a bowl. The dough should be sticky and hold together. If it seems too moist, add 1 tablespoon flour.

2. Bring a pot of water to a boil. Scoop a large serving spoon full of dough and, using a sharp knife, slice small pieces of dough (½ inch) into the boiling water.

3. After the dough rises to the top of the water, cook approximately 1 minute longer.

4. Remove with a slotted spoon and place in a bowl.

5. Before serving, melt 2 tablespoons butter in a skillet and sauté the spaetzle until golden.

KREPLACH

3 cups shredded leftover pot-roasted meat
1 leek, trimmed, rinsed, and chopped
1 garlic clove, minced
1 small carrot, cut up
1 small celery rib, cut up
½ teaspoon coarsely ground black pepper
1 tablespoon olive oil
1 Basic Pasta Recipe (page 25)
6 cups chicken broth

Kreplach are Jewish dumplings. People shape them differently, but they usually look like ravioli or won tons.

1. Grind together all the ingredients, except the oil, pasta, and broth, in a blender, food processor, or meat grinder.
2. Heat the oil in a skillet and cook the mixture over low heat for 5 minutes.
3. Remove to a bowl and refrigerate while you prepare the dough.
4. Divide the dough into quarters and roll out to about ⅛-inch thickness. Cut into 2½–3-inch squares.
5. Place 1½ teaspoons of the filling in the center of each square, fold the dough into a triangle, and seal the edges.
6. Bring the broth to a boil and drop the kreplach into it. Cook for 10–15 minutes. Serve in soup bowls with the broth.

THE POWER OF PASTA

BAKED PASTA

Most pasta dishes can be completed without ever turning on the oven — which many people consider another important advantage of these recipes. It's true that next to the recipes in the preceding chapter, this chapter's recipes are probably the most time-consuming in the book (except for the Quick Lasagna recipe, page 49) — and they are worth every minute of that time.

Along with my favorite recipe for Traditional Lasagna (page 48), you'll find two interesting and exceptionally good lasagna variations. Be sure to try the unusual and wonderfully light Pasta Soufflé (page 52)!

MANICOTTI

4 cups tomato sauce
1 pound low-fat ricotta
¾ cup grated Parmesan cheese
½ cup cream or half-and-half
6 scallions (white plus about 2 inches of
    green), grated
¼ cup chopped parsley
¼ teaspoon mace
⅛ teaspoon finely ground black pepper
12 manicotti shells, cooked according to the
    package directions
½ cup heavy cream (optional)
¼ cup grated Parmesan cheese

The filling for the manicotti can be made at least one day ahead of time. It can be used to stuff cannelloni, ravioli, and jumbo shells with excellent results.

1. Preheat the oven to 375° F. Butter a 9 x 13 baking dish.
2. Pour ¼ cup of tomato sauce in the baking dish to cover the bottom.
3. Mix the remaining ingredients, except the shells, the cream, and the ¼ cup Parmesan, until thoroughly combined.
4. Stuff the cooked manicotti shells and place them in the baking dish.
5. Cover with the remaining tomato sauce. Pour the heavy cream over the top.
6. Cover the dish with aluminum foil and bake for 15 minutes.
7. Remove the foil, sprinkle with ¼ cup Parmesan and return to the oven for 10 more minutes. Serve.

TRADITIONAL LASAGNA

PREPARATION TIME: 60 MINUTES   BAKING TIME: 30 MINUTES   YIELD: 8–10 SERVINGS

½ pound Italian sausage meat
½ pound lean ground beef
2 garlic cloves, crushed or minced
1 teaspoon dried oregano
1 teaspoon dried basil
¼ teaspoon coarsely ground black pepper
3 cups chopped tomatoes, or 1 28-ounce can
    crushed tomatoes
4 cups part-skim ricotta or dry cottage cheese
1 cup grated Parmesan cheese
2 large eggs, beaten
¼ cup low-fat milk
½ teaspoon mace
¼ teaspoon finely ground pepper
1 pound part-skim mozzarella, grated
¼ cup chopped parsley
12–16 lasagna noodles, cooked according to
    the package directions and drained
¼ cup grated Parmesan cheese

I frequently prepare a lasagna dish ahead of time and either refrigerate it for a day, or freeze it for a later date. From a refrigerated state, it goes into a pre-heated 375° F. oven for 45 minutes; from the freezer it will need 1–1¼ hours. Keep covered for the first half hour to prevent the sauce from drying out.

1. Preheat the oven to 375° F. and grease a 9 x 13 baking dish.
2. Break up and brown the sausage meat in a skillet over medium heat for 2–3 minutes. Remove and drain off the excess fat.
3. Add the ground beef to the skillet, break it up and brown it for 2–3 minutes.
4. Add the garlic and stir for 1 minute.
5. Return the sausage meat to the skillet and add the oregano, basil, coarsely ground pepper, and chopped or crushed tomatoes. Stir to combine and simmer on low for 15–20 minutes.
6. In a large bowl, combine the ricotta, 1 cup Parmesan cheese, eggs, low-fat milk, mace, and finely ground pepper.
7. Combine the grated mozzarella and chopped parsley in a separate bowl.

THE POWER OF PASTA

8. Place a layer of lasagna noodles in the baking dish and spread with one-third of the ricotta mixture, followed by one-third of the meat sauce and one-third of the mozzarella and parsley. Repeat two more times (so that there are three layers) and sprinkle the ¼ cup Parmesan over the top.
9. Bake for 30 minutes, or until the center is steaming.

ANN KOJIS'S QUICK LASAGNA

PREPARATION TIME: 20 MINUTES   BAKING TIME: 25 MINUTES   YIELD: 6 SERVINGS

1 pound pasta shells
8 ounces part-skim ricotta cheese
6 ounces part-skim mozzarella, grated
¼ cup grated Parmesan cheese
4–6 cups tomato sauce
¼ cup grated Parmesan cheese

1. Preheat the oven to 350° F. and butter a 9 x 13 baking dish.
2. Cook the shells al dente according to the package directions. Drain and rinse under cold water.
3. In a large mixing bowl, combine the ricotta, two-thirds of the grated mozzarella, and ¼ cup Parmesan cheese. Fold in the cooled shells and spoon the mixture into the baking dish.
4. Top with the tomato sauce and sprinkle with the remaining mozzarella and another ¼ cup Parmesan cheese.
5. Bake for 25 minutes or until the center is steaming.

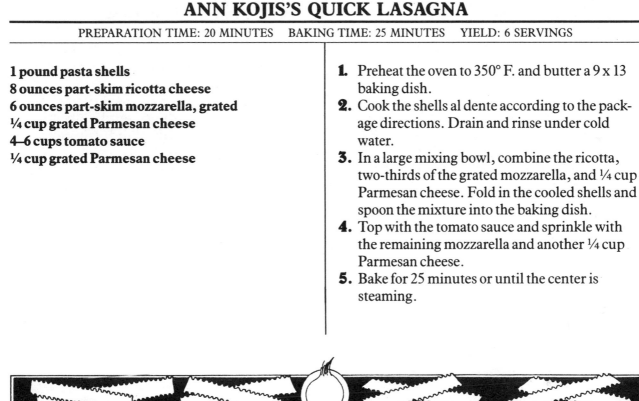

EASY EGGPLANT LASAGNA

PREPARATION TIME: 60 MINUTES   BAKING TIME: 30 MINUTES   YIELD: 8–10 SERVINGS

¼ cup olive oil

2 medium-size onions, thinly sliced (4 cups)

1½ pounds eggplant, peeled and cubed (8 cups)

4 garlic cloves, crushed or minced

1 tablespoon dried thyme

1 tablespoon dried oregano

½ teaspoon coarsely ground black pepper

1 28-ounce can peeled plum tomatoes in
    purée, roughly chopped

3 cups part-skim ricotta

1 cup grated Parmesan cheese

1 cup chopped parsley

12–16 lasagna noodles, cooked according to the
    package directions and drained

1 pound part-skim mozzarella, thinly sliced

½ cup grated Romano cheese

1. Preheat the oven to 375° F. and grease a 9 x 13 baking dish.
2. Heat the olive oil in a large skillet and sauté the onions for 5 minutes.
3. Add the eggplant cubes, garlic, and seasonings. Stir and cook for 10 minutes.
4. Add the chopped tomatoes and cook for 10 more minutes. Remove from the heat.
5. Mix the ricotta, Parmesan, and parsley in a large bowl.
6. Place a layer of lasagna noodles in the baking dish and spread with one-third of the ricotta mixture, followed by one-third of the eggplant, and one-third of the sliced mozzarella.
7. Repeat two more times (so that there are three layers) and sprinkle the final layer of mozzarella with the grated Romano.
8. Bake for 30 minutes, or until the center is steaming.

CHICKEN-SPINACH LASAGNA

PREPARATION TIME: 45 MINUTES   BAKING TIME: 45 MINUTES   YIELD: 8–10 SERVINGS

1 cup grated **Parmesan cheese**

3 cups part-skim ricotta

2 cups cooked, chopped spinach (2 10-ounce frozen packages, thawed and drained)

1 cup chopped parsley

4 large garlic cloves, crushed or minced

1½ teaspoons mace

½ teaspoon coarsely ground black pepper

1 tablespoon dried oregano

12–16 lasagna noodles, cooked according to the package directions and drained

4 cups slivered cooked chicken

1 28-ounce can crushed tomatoes, or 1½ cups chopped fresh tomatoes plus 1 cup tomato purée

3 cups grated part-skim mozzarella

½ cup grated **Romano cheese**

This is a party winner in every way. Not only can it be prepared ahead of time, so all you have to do is heat it and make an accompanying salad, but the flavor is unbeatable, and the layers are an attractive green and cream.

1. Preheat the oven to 350° F. and grease a 9 x 13 baking dish.
2. In a large bowl, beat together the Parmesan cheese, ricotta, spinach, parsley, garlic, mace, pepper, and oregano.
3. Make a layer of noodles in the dish and spread with one-third of the ricotta mixture, followed by one-third of the chicken, one-third of the crushed tomatoes, and one-third of the mozzarella.
4. Repeat the layers two more times (so that there are three layers) and sprinkle the top with the Romano cheese.
5. Bake for 45 minutes, or until the center is steaming.

PASTA SOUFFLÉ

8 ounces green fettuccine noodles
1 tablespoon olive oil
2 tablespoons butter
3 tablespoons all-purpose flour
1 cup low-fat milk
½ cup grated or crumbled hard cheese such as cheddar, bleu, or Parmesan
½ teaspoon coarsely ground black pepper
4 large eggs, separated
pinch cream of tartar

1. Preheat the oven to 375° F. and butter a 2-quart soufflé dish or other deep baking dish.
2. Cook the noodles according to the package directions, drain, and toss with the oil.
3. Melt the butter in a small saucepan, stir in the flour, and cook for 1 minute.
4. Gradually add the milk, stirring constantly, until the mixture is smooth and thickened.
5. Add the cheese and pepper. Cook for 2 minutes, stirring constantly, until the cheese is thoroughly blended. Remove from the heat.
6. Beat the egg whites with a pinch of cream of tartar, until stiff peaks form.
7. Beat the egg yolks into the cheese mixture, stir in the noodles, and then fold in one-third of the egg whites. Fold this, in turn, into the remaining egg whites in the large bowl.
8. Pour the mixture into the buttered baking dish and bake for 45 minutes. Serve immediately.

BAKED MACARONI RICOTTA

2 cups leftover cooked pasta (with or
    without sauce)
1 cup diced ham
2 large eggs, beaten
1 cup low-fat milk
1 cup low-fat ricotta or cottage cheese
½ teaspoon mace
¼ teaspoon coarsely ground black pepper
¼ teaspoon powdered mustard
½ cup chopped chives or scallion greens
⅓ cup grated Parmesan or Romano cheese

1. Preheat the oven to 325° F. and lightly grease a 2-quart baking dish.
2. Mix the pasta and ham. Place in the baking dish.
3. Mix the eggs, milk, cottage cheese, mace, pepper, mustard, and chives. Pour over the macaroni.
4. Sprinkle with the grated Parmesan and bake for 50 minutes. Serve.

PASTA WITH LEGUMES

Dried beans and peas are rich in protein, iron, calcium, phosphorus, potassium, and B vitamins. Their fat content is not only low, it is polyunsaturated, which helps to lower levels of cholesterol in the blood. However, it is necessary to combine beans with a little meat, whole grain bread, rice, or pasta in order to create a meal of balanced protein (see pages 5–6).

Dried beans must be soaked for several hours (usually overnight) before they can be cooked. This time can be reduced from 8 to 2 hours (or less) if the beans are covered with cold water, boiled for 10 minutes, drained, and then soaked in cold water for 1–2 hours. However, I find it very convenient to measure dried beans into a pot, cover them with cold water, and leave them to soak overnight or through the day.

Leftover pasta is a natural for soups, and there are some excellent ones in this chapter. After the soup has finished cooking, add 1 cup of pasta (cut longer pieces into a manageable size) and heat on low for 5–10 minutes, just until the pasta is heated through.

LAMB, BEAN, AND DITALINI SOUP

PREPARATION TIME: 10 MINUTES   COOKING TIME: 3½–4 HOURS   YIELD: 6–8 SERVINGS

1 cup dried navy beans
4 lamb shanks, fat removed
1 cup sliced celery
2–3 garlic cloves, crushed or minced
½ teaspoon coarsely ground black pepper
2 teaspoons dried thyme
2 teaspoons dried leaf sage
1 cup tomato juice
2 cups chicken stock
½–1 cup red wine
½ cup ditalini or small specialty shape

1. Bring 4 cups of water to a boil. Add the navy beans and cook for 10 minutes. Remove from the heat and let the beans soak.
2. Place the lamb shanks, celery, seasonings, and liquids in a 6-quart Dutch oven, cover, and bring to a gentle boil. Reduce the heat to low and simmer for 3 hours, or until the lamb is tender.
3. Drain the beans after 2 hours and cover with 4 cups of fresh cold water. Bring to a boil. Then reduce the heat and simmer, cover askew, for 1½–2 hours, until the beans are tender. Drain. You will have 2 cups of cooked beans.
4. In the meantime, cook the ditalini in 4 cups boiling water for 8 minutes. Drain and add to the lamb shanks along with the cooked navy beans. Simmer for 15 minutes to heat through. Serve hot.

PASTA WITH LEGUMES

CHICKEN-GARBANZO SOUP

COOKING TIME: 20 MINUTES   YIELD: 4 SERVINGS

8 ounces cheese tortellini or elbow macaroni
4 cups oxtail soup
2 cups roughly cubed, cooked chicken
2 cups cooked garbanzo beans or kidney beans

I like to use homemade oxtail soup as the base for this soup, but there's nothing to stop you from trying commercial, dried oxtail soup or substituting tomato soup, chicken broth, or any other soup that you have on hand. If you make the oxtail soup from scratch, add 6 hours to the cooking time and make it a day ahead — it has to be refrigerated overnight. The oxtail soup recipe makes 4 cups.

I use the commercial frozen type of tortellini for this recipe.

1. Cook the tortellini according to the package directions, and drain it.
2. Slowly bring the oxtail soup to a boil in a 4-quart pot. Then reduce the heat to a simmer and add the tortellini, chicken, and beans.
3. Simmer for 10 minutes. Serve hot.

OXTAIL SOUP

1 pound oxtails, rolled in flour
1 carrot
1 medium-size onion
½ teaspoon dried thyme
1 teaspoon dried sage
¼ teaspoon coarsely ground black pepper

1. Preheat the oven to 400° F. and oil a shallow baking dish.
2. Spread the floured oxtail pieces in the baking dish and roast in the preheated oven for 20 minutes. Remove the oxtails from the oven and discard any fat.

3. Place the oxtails in a 4-quart pot and cover with water.
4. Add the remaining ingredients and bring to a boil.
5. Cover the pot (leaving the lid askew) and simmer for 6 hours.

6. Strain the soup through a colander into a bowl. Discard the vegetables and the oxtail bones.
7. Refrigerate overnight and remove the thick layer of fat the next day.

BEANS AND PASTA WITH FRESH TOMATO SAUCE

PREPARATION TIME: 10 MINUTES   COOKING TIME: 30 MINUTES   YIELD: 4 SERVINGS

2 tablespoons olive oil
1 small onion, chopped (½ cup)
2 garlic cloves, crushed or minced
2 bell peppers, chopped (2 cups)
3 cups Tomato Sauce II (page 125)
2 teaspoons dried basil
2 teaspoons dried oregano
½ teaspoon coarsely ground black pepper
2 cups cooked beans (cannelini, kidney,
    garbanzo, etc.)
1 pound cut, ribbed ziti

1. Heat the oil in a skillet and sauté the onion, garlic, and bell peppers for 10 minutes.
2. Add the tomato sauce, basil, oregano, pepper, and cooked beans. Bring the sauce to a bubble, reduce the heat, and simmer for 15–20 minutes.
3. Cook the ziti according to the package directions. Drain and top with the sauce. Serve immediately.

PASTA PILAF GARBANZO

2 tablespoons olive oil
½ cup finely chopped onion
¾ cup finely chopped walnuts or
    blanched almonds
½ teaspoon coarsely ground black pepper
1 tablespoon dried basil
½ cup cracked bulgur wheat or brown rice
1 cup stock, no-salt V-8 Juice, or water
1 cup cooked garbanzo beans or other
    cooked beans
½ cup orzo pasta
1 tablespoon olive oil
¼ cup grated Parmesan or Romano cheese

1. Heat 2 tablespoons olive oil in a skillet and sauté the onion, walnuts, pepper, and basil for 5 minutes.
2. Add the bulgur wheat and sauté for 2 minutes.
3. Pour in the stock, cover the skillet, and cook for 15 minutes, until most of the liquid has been absorbed and the bulgur is al dente tender.
4. Stir in the cooked beans and heat for 10 minutes on low.
5. Cook the orzo according to the package directions. Drain and mix with 1 tablespoon olive oil.
6. Combine everything in a large, warmed serving dish and serve sprinkled with Parmesan cheese.

FARMHOUSE SOUP

PREPARATION TIME: 10 MINUTES   COOKING TIME: 1¾ HOURS   YIELD: 4 SERVINGS

¼ cup dried split peas
¼ cup lentils
¼ cup pearl barley
2 medium-size carrots, chopped fine
   (about 1½ cups)
2 small celery ribs, chopped fine (about 1 cup)
1 large onion, chopped fine (about 2 cups)
1 teaspoon dried basil
1 teaspoon dried oregano
¼ teaspoon coarsely ground black pepper,
   or to taste
2 garlic cloves, crushed or minced
8 cups water
¾ cup elbow macaroni, tubettini, or ditalini
1 tablespoon Basil Pesto, page 138 (optional)

When you prepare the celery, wash a large piece of celery top and throw it into the soup for extra seasoning.

1. Place the dried peas, lentils, barley, chopped vegetables, herbs, pepper, and garlic in a 6-quart pot and cover with the 8 cups water.
2. Bring to a boil, cover (leaving the lid askew), and reduce the heat. Simmer for 1½ hours.
3. Throw in the macaroni and cook for 15 minutes.
4. Stir in the pesto just before serving, if desired.

VEGETABLE, TUBETTINI, AND BEAN SOUP

PREPARATION TIME: 10 MINUTES   COOKING TIME: 45 MINUTES   YIELD: 4–6 SERVINGS

6 cups chicken stock
1 cup carrot juice
1 cup tomato juice
1 cup sliced celery
1 cup thinly sliced carrots
½ teaspoon coarsely ground black pepper
1 teaspoon dried basil
1 cup fresh or frozen green beans
2 cups cooked cannelini beans
¾ cup tubettini macaroni, cooked according to
   the package directions (2 cups cooked)

I make my chicken stock by simmering several chicken backs with an onion, a carrot, and a rib of celery for 2 hours or more. This broth is then strained, refrigerated, and the fat scraped off when congealed.

1. Place the stock, juices, celery, carrots, pepper, and basil in a 4-quart pot. Cover and cook at a gentle boil for 30 minutes.
2. Add the green beans, cannelini, and tubettini and cook for 15 minutes longer. Serve.

THE POWER OF PASTA

MEXICAN BEANS AND MACARONI

PREPARATION TIME: 10 MINUTES   COOKING TIME: 10 MINUTES   YIELD: 4 SERVINGS

¾ pound ditalini or elbow macaroni
1 16-ounce can pinto or red kidney beans,
    including liquid
1 medium-size red onion, chopped (1 cup)
1 jalapeño pepper, chopped (optional)
1 large red bell pepper, chopped (1¼ cups)
¼ cup olive oil
1 tablespoon wine vinegar
¼ cup "mild" vegetable taco sauce
2 garlic cloves, crushed or minced
1 teaspoon chili powder
1 teaspoon cumin powder
1 cup grated Monterey Jack or cheddar cheese

1. Cook the macaroni in boiling water according
   to the package directions and drain.
2. Place the beans, onion, jalapeño pepper, and
   bell pepper in a large serving bowl. Add the
   hot macaroni.
3. Combine the olive oil, vinegar, taco sauce, garlic, and chili and cumin powders and pour over
   the macaroni and beans. Toss together.
4. Sprinkle with the grated cheese and serve immediately or refrigerate and serve chilled.

PASTA-AND-MEAT ENTRÉES

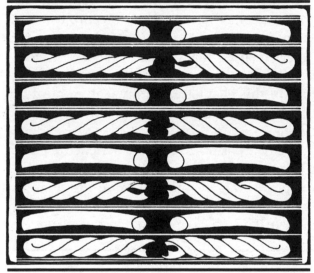

This chapter started out to be meat entrées with pasta side dishes, but gradually the pasta became more and more central in the recipes. Nevertheless, although there are other recipes that contain meat scattered throughout the chapters of this book, the recipes in this chapter generally feature meat as the dominant ingredient — next to the pasta, that is.

We're accustomed to the experience of pasta and meatballs, and you'll find two excellent recipes in this chapter. But don't hesitate to try the more unusual combinations of pasta with turkey, chicken livers, and venison!

ANN NAPPI'S MACARONI WITH MEAT AND SAUCE

PREPARATION TIME: 10 MINUTES   COOKING TIME: 1½–2 HOURS   YIELD: 4–6 SERVINGS

1 cup bread stuffing, or 3 slices stale Italian bread
2–4 tablespoons water
1½ pounds ground chuck
1 large egg, beaten
salt and pepper to taste
2–4 tablespoons chopped parsley
¼ cup grated Romano cheese
3 garlic cloves, crushed or minced
2 tablespoons olive oil
½ pound whole Italian sausages (each about 6 inches long)
½ pound chuck filet, cut in 2-inch pieces
1 garlic clove, crushed or minced
salt and pepper to taste
1 tablespoon dried basil
1 35-ounce can whole tomatoes
1 6-ounce can tomato paste
1 pound macaroni (spaghetti, linguini, or perciatelle)
4 tablespoons grated Romano cheese

1. Place the stuffing or bread slices in a large bowl and moisten with the water.
2. Add the ground chuck, egg, salt and pepper, parsley, ¼ cup Romano, and 3 crushed garlic cloves. Mix everything together and form into meatballs.
3. Heat the oil in a large skillet and brown the sausages, chuck pieces, and 1 garlic clove.
4. Add salt and pepper and the basil.
5. Process the tomatoes in a blender and add them to the pan with the tomato paste. Thin with a little water, if necessary.
6. Add the meatballs and simmer for 1½–2 hours.
7. Cook the macaroni in boiling water according to the package directions. Drain and place in a large bowl. Top with the Romano cheese and the sauce. Serve immediately.

POT ROAST WITH EGG NOODLES

PREPARATION TIME: 25 MINUTES   COOKING TIME: 3½ HOURS   YIELD: 6–8 SERVINGS

4 pounds chuck pot roast
2 tablespoons flour
2 tablespoons vegetable oil
1 large onion, sliced
2–4 garlic cloves, crushed or minced
½ teaspoon coarsely ground black pepper
2 teaspoons dried leaf sage
2 teaspoons dried thyme
2 tablespoons flour
1½ cups red wine
½ cup apple juice
½ cup tomato purée
3 carrots, sliced
3 celery ribs, sliced
1 pound large, flat egg noodles
2 tablespoons butter

1. Roll the pot roast in 2 tablespoons flour.
2. Pour the vegetable oil into a Dutch oven and place over medium heat.
3. Brown the meat in the oil on all sides for 3–4 minutes. Remove to a plate.
4. Add the onion, garlic, pepper, sage, thyme, and 2 tablespoons flour to the pot. Stir and sauté for 5 minutes.
5. Combine the wine, apple juice, and tomato purée. Stir into the onion mixture.
6. Bring the liquids to a boil, reduce the heat, and return the pot roast to the pan.
7. Cover the pot, leaving the lid slightly askew. Simmer for 2½ hours.
8. Add the carrots and celery and simmer for 1 hour longer.
9. About 15 minutes before the pot roast finishes cooking, place the noodles in a large pot of boiling water and cook according to the package directions.
10. Drain the noodles and toss with the butter.
11. Remove the pot roast from the heat. Slice the roast and place it on top of the noodles on a serving platter. Spoon the vegetables and some gravy over the top. Pour the rest of the gravy into a container and serve on the side.

TENDERLOIN OF PORK
WITH FUSILLI AND PIQUANT TOMATO SAUCE

PREPARATION TIME: 10 MINUTES
COOKING TIME: 20 MINUTES FOR PORK, 10 MINUTES FOR PASTA AND SAUCE   YIELD: 4 SERVINGS

1½ pounds pork tenderloin
⅓ cup olive oil
1 tablespoon wine vinegar
2 garlic cloves, crushed or minced
1 tablespoon dried oregano
1 tablespoon dried basil

Pork tenderloin is about 1½ inches in diameter and 1–1½ inches thick. Instead of barbecuing or broiling, you can cut it into ½-inch-thick slices and simmer it for 20 minutes in the sauce, if you wish.

1. Put the pork tenderloin in a shallow dish and cover it with the rest of the ingredients. Turn to coat. (I usually leave it to marinate while the barbecue coals are heating to a grey stage — about 30 minutes.)
2. Place on the grill or under a broiler and cook 6 inches from the heat. Turn after 10 minutes and continue cooking 10 minutes longer.
3. Slice into ½-inch-thick pieces and drizzle with any remaining marinade.

FUSILLI AND SAUCE

12 ounces fusilli (curly spaghetti)
1½ cups tomato purée
½ cup cream
2 large garlic cloves, crushed or minced
⅛ teaspoon cayenne pepper, or several dashes
   Tabasco sauce (to taste)
1 tablespoon dried oregano

1. Cook the fusilli in 4 quarts boiling water, according to the package directions.
2. Combine the rest of the ingredients in a 2-quart saucepan and heat on medium for 5 minutes, or until hot.
3. Drain the fusilli, place on a warm serving platter, and cover with the sauce.
4. Serve immediately with the pork slices.

THE GIORGIOS' SICILIAN VENISON CASSEROLE

PREPARATION TIME: 30 MINUTES   BAKING TIME: 35 MINUTES   YIELD: 6–8 SERVINGS

1 tablespoon olive oil
1½ pounds ground venison
1 large onion, finely chopped
4 medium-size carrots, finely chopped
¼ pound mushrooms, sliced
6 ounces tomato paste
⅔ cup dry sherry
1 16-ounce can whole plum tomatoes
1½ teaspoons dried basil
1½ teaspoons dried oregano
½ teaspoon coarsely ground black pepper
½ teaspoon garlic powder
6 ounces elbow macaroni, cooked al dente
  and drained
10–12 ounces cooked, chopped spinach, drained
6 ounces grated cheddar cheese (1½ cups)
½ cup grated Parmesan cheese

I met Joe Giorgio, a detective with the Ossining, New York, Police Department, when I was a reporter for a local newspaper. He gave his wife Kathleen's cooking such rave reviews that I asked for a couple of her recipes. This is one of them.

1. Preheat the oven to 375° F. and grease a 9 x 13 baking dish.
2. Heat the olive oil in a large skillet and brown the ground venison for 5 minutes, stirring frequently.
3. Push the meat to one side and add the onion and carrots. Sauté for 5 minutes.
4. Add the sliced mushrooms and stir everything together.
5. Combine the tomato paste and sherry and add to the pan with the plum tomatoes and seasonings.
6. Simmer for 30 minutes.
7. While the sauce is cooking, mix the elbows, spinach, and cheddar cheese together. Place in the bottom of the baking dish.
8. Top with the meat sauce and sprinkle with the grated Parmesan.
9. Bake for 35–40 minutes.

SAUSAGE MEATBALLS WITH ZITI

PREPARATION TIME: 20 MINUTES   COOKING TIME: 30 MINUTES   YIELD: 4 SERVINGS

1 pound beef, finely ground
1 pound pork, finely ground
2–4 garlic cloves, crushed or minced
6 scallions, including green, finely sliced
1 teaspoon mace
1 teaspoon crumbled leaf sage
2 teaspoons dried thyme
½ teaspoon dried rosemary leaves
½ teaspoon coarsely ground black pepper
2 cups fresh oatmeal, or whole grain
  breadcrumbs (about 4 large slices of bread)
¾ cup liquid (tomato juice, stock, wine, or
  no-salt V-8 Juice)
1 tablespoon vegetable oil

I use half of the meatballs (about twenty 1-inch meatballs) with this recipe and freeze the other half for another night. Or I make sausage patties and broil them for breakfast.

1. Place all the ingredients except the oil in a large bowl and mix with your hands or with a fork.
2. Form the mixture into balls approximately 1-inch across.
3. Heat the oil in a skillet and sauté 10 meatballs at a time for 1–2 minutes, rolling them around to sear them on all sides. Remove to a dish.

TOMATO SAUCE

1 tablespoon olive oil
1 medium-size onion, chopped fine
1 28-ounce can whole tomatoes, puréed
  to make 3½ cups
1 teaspoon dried thyme
1 teaspoon mace
¼ cup cream (optional)
1 pound cut ziti

1. Heat the oil in a skillet and sauté the chopped onion for 5 minutes.
2. Stir in the rest of the ingredients, except the ziti, and heat for 5 minutes.
3. Add 20 meatballs, cover the skillet, and simmer for 15–20 minutes.
4. While the sauce is simmering, cook the ziti according to the package directions. Drain and serve with the sauce and meatballs.

TURKEY BREAST WITH PASTA AND MUSHROOM SAUCE

PREPARATION TIME: 10 MINUTES FOR TURKEY, 10 MINUTES FOR SAUCE
COOKING TIME: 1½ HOURS FOR TURKEY, 10 MINUTES FOR SAUCE   YIELD: 4–6 SERVINGS

1 medium-size celery rib, sliced
1 medium-size carrot, sliced
1 medium-size onion, sliced
1 whole turkey breast (about 2 pounds)
1 teaspoon olive oil
1 cup white wine
1 teaspoon dried thyme
¼ teaspoon coarsely ground black pepper

1. Preheat the oven to 400° F.
2. Place the sliced vegetables in the bottom of a roasting dish.
3. Rub the turkey breast with the olive oil, and place it on top of the vegetables (skin-side up).
4. Pour the wine over the top, sprinkle with thyme and pepper, and place the dish on the top shelf of the hot oven.
5. Roast for 40 minutes. Cover and continue cooking for another 30 minutes.
6. Uncover and cook for 20 minutes.

MUSHROOM SAUCE

1 pound rigati mostaccioli (cut ziti, twists,
   or penne)
2 tablespoons olive oil
3 large garlic cloves, crushed or minced
2 red bell peppers, chopped
1 pound mushrooms, sliced
1½ teaspoons dried thyme
½ teaspoon coarsely ground black pepper
½ cup tomato sauce
½ cup cream, or ¼ cup sour cream diluted with
   ¼ cup low-fat milk
½ cup chopped parsley
¼ cup grated Parmesan cheese

1. Cook the pasta in boiling water according to
   the package directions.
2. Pour the olive oil into a skillet and heat on
   medium.
3. Add the garlic and chopped bell peppers and
   sauté for 5 minutes.
4. Add the sliced mushrooms, thyme, and pepper. Cook for 2 minutes.
5. Pour in the tomato sauce and cream. Heat on
   low for 3 minutes.
6. Drain the pasta, place in a warm serving bowl,
   and toss with the Parmesan cheese, the parsley, and the mushroom sauce. Serve along
   with the turkey.

PASTA-AND-MEAT ENTRÉES

THE GIORGIOS' VENISON AND MUSHROOM SAUCE OVER VERMICELLI

PREPARATION TIME: 10 MINUTES   COOKING TIME: 20 MINUTES   YIELD: 4 SERVINGS

3 tablespoons butter
½ pound venison, cut in thin strips
½ pound mushrooms, thinly sliced
¾ cup tomato juice
½ teaspoon dried sage
⅛ teaspoon ground nutmeg
⅓ cup cream
¼ cup chopped parsley
8 ounces vermicelli
½ cup grated Parmesan cheese

1. Melt the butter in a skillet and lightly brown the venison strips for 2–3 minutes.
2. Stir in the sliced mushrooms and cook for 2 minutes.
3. Add the tomato juice, sage, nutmeg, cream, and parsley. Cook for 5–10 minutes. Time will vary depending on the tenderness of the venison strips.
4. Cook the vermicelli according to the package directions, drain, place on a warmed dish, and sprinkle with the Parmesan cheese. Top with the meat sauce.

CHICKEN LIVERS HUNTER STYLE

PREPARATION TIME: 20 MINUTES   COOKING TIME: 30 MINUTES   YIELD: 4 SERVINGS

4 tablespoons olive oil

1½ cups chopped bell peppers
(2 medium-size peppers)

3 large garlic cloves, crushed or minced

⅔ cup sliced scallions (6 large scallions,
including green)

8 ounces mushrooms, sliced

½ cup chopped parsley

¼ cup fresh oregano leaves

½ teaspoon coarsely ground black pepper

¼ teaspoon hot red pepper flakes

1 pound firm chicken livers, separated and
cut in half

1 28-ounce can crushed tomatoes, or 3 cups fresh
chopped tomatoes plus ½ cup tomato purée

1 pound linguini, cooked according to
package directions

½–1 cup grated Romano cheese

Hunter sauce is another name for cacciatore, which is a hearty blend of mushrooms, garlic, and tomato, usually served over meat. Red bell peppers seem to work better than green.

I use my 13-inch, black iron skillet for this recipe because it's the biggest one I possess.

1. Pour 2 tablespoons of the olive oil into a skillet and place over medium heat.
2. Add the chopped bell peppers, garlic, and scallions. Sauté for 3 minutes.
3. Stir in the mushrooms, parsley, oregano, pepper, and hot pepper flakes. Cook for 2 minutes and push to one side of the pan.
4. Add 2 more tablespoons olive oil, and when the oil is hot, add the chicken livers and stir and turn for 3–4 minutes.
5. Pour in the chopped tomatoes, mix all the ingredients together, lower the heat, and simmer for 20 minutes.
6. Serve over the linguini, with Romano cheese on the side.

PASTA-AND-MEAT ENTRÉES

PASTA
AND SEAFOOD

Seafood and pasta, it seems to me, should be listed among the world's greatest gastronomic combinations. Like all other pasta recipes, the seafood recipes lend themselves to endless experimentation and substitution. When one type of seafood is not available, another can be used with excellent results. If shrimp or scallops seem too high priced at certain times of the year, then it's perfectly okay to substitute cubed monkfish or cod. (If you do use shrimp and want to stretch them to feed four rather than two, slice them in half lengthwise and cut their cooking time in half also.) Many of the following recipes can be prepared and cooked in just half an hour.

ZITI WITH TUNA SAUCE

1 pound cut ziti or penne
2 tablespoons olive oil
2 garlic cloves, crushed or minced
1 large sweet red bell pepper, chopped fine
2 pounds fresh tomatoes, chopped, or
   1 28-ounce can crushed tomatoes
1 6½-ounce can tuna packed in water, drained
¼ cup fresh oregano, chopped, or
   1 tablespoon dried oregano
½ teaspoon coarsely ground black pepper
½ cup chopped parsley
1 cup grated mozzarella

1. Cook the pasta according to the package directions.
2. Heat the olive oil in a skillet over medium heat and add the garlic. Sauté for about 10 seconds.
3. Add the chopped peppers and sauté for 2 minutes.
4. Add the chopped tomatoes, reduce the heat, and simmer for 10 minutes.
5. Using a wooden spoon, crush the tuna into the sauce. Stir in the oregano, pepper, and ¼ cup of the chopped parsley. Simmer for 10 more minutes.
6. Combine the grated mozzarella and the remaining ¼ cup of chopped parsley.
7. Drain the pasta (stir in 1 tablespoon olive oil or butter if desired) and toss with the mozzarella and parsley. Turn into a large, warm serving dish, top with the hot tuna sauce, and serve.

FETTUCCINE SHRIMP JAMBALAYA

PREPARATION TIME: 15 MINUTES   COOKING TIME: 20 MINUTES   YIELD: 4 SERVINGS

8 ounces fettuccine noodles
⅓ cup olive oil or vegetable oil
1 green bell pepper, chopped (1 cup)
1 large onion, chopped (2 cups)
1 large celery rib, chopped (1 cup)
3 large garlic cloves, minced
1 bay leaf
2 teaspoons dried thyme
¼ teaspoon coarsely ground black pepper
⅛ teaspoon cayenne pepper
1 teaspoon mace
¼ cup chopped parsley
2 cups chopped tomatoes, fresh or canned
8 ounces ½-inch-thick ham, cubed
1 pound medium-size shrimp, shelled and
    cleaned, or ¾ pound shelled
    medium-size shrimp

This is a superb way to stretch a shrimp dinner. If you are serving someone with an extra hearty appetite, you can use 12 ounces of noodles instead of 8.

1. Cook the noodles in boiling water according to the package directions.
2. Heat the oil in a large skillet and sauté the bell pepper, onion, celery, and garlic for 10 minutes.
3. Drain the noodles when they are cooked.
4. Add the seasonings, parsley, and tomatoes to the skillet. Cook for 5 minutes.
5. Add the ham and the shrimp to the skillet and cook for 3 minutes.
6. Add the drained noodles to the shrimp mixture and heat through for 2 minutes or so.
7. Turn onto a warmed platter and serve immediately.

TARRAGON SHRIMP WITH TWISTS

PREPARATION TIME: 10 MINUTES   COOKING TIME: 15 MINUTES   YIELD: 4 SERVINGS

1 pound rotelle (twists, cut fusilli)
2 tablespoons olive oil
2 large shallots, chopped (about 2 tablespoons)
2 garlic cloves, crushed or minced
2 teaspoons dried oregano
1 teaspoon dried tarragon
⅛ teaspoon cayenne pepper
1 pound shelled, medium-size shrimp, cut in half
2 cups tomato sauce
1 cup pitted black olives, sliced

For this recipe, buy 1¼ pounds of shrimp with shells. You always lose about ¼ pound when you shell shrimp.

1. Cook the pasta according to the package directions.
2. Pour the olive oil into a skillet and place over medium heat.
3. Add the shallots, garlic, oregano, tarragon, and cayenne pepper.
4. Stir together and immediately add the shrimp pieces. Coat them with the herb mixture and stir and cook for 1 minute.
5. Pour in the tomato sauce and sliced olives. Stir and simmer on low for 10 minutes.
6. Drain the twists, place them in a warm serving bowl, and cover them with the sauce. Serve immediately.

SHRIMP AND SCALLOPS WITH LINGUINI

PREPARATION TIME: 10 MINUTES   COOKING TIME: 20 MINUTES   YIELD: 2 SERVINGS

8 ounces linguini
2 tablespoons olive oil
1 cup watercress leaves, chopped
1 red bell pepper, chopped very fine
2 garlic cloves, crushed or minced
½ cup white wine
1 cup tomato sauce
½ cup cream or half-and-half
½ teaspoon mace
½ teaspoon coarsely ground black pepper
¾ pound medium-size shrimp, shelled and cleaned, or ½ pound shelled medium-size shrimp
½ pound bay scallops

1. Cook the linguini in boiling water according to the package directions. Then drain and keep warm.
2. Heat the olive oil in a skillet and sauté the watercress, bell pepper, and garlic for 3 minutes over low heat.
3. Add the wine and boil for 1 minute. (On an electric stove, you can cook the wine on low for about 3 minutes to evaporate the alcohol.)
4. Add the tomato sauce and simmer for 10 minutes.
5. Stir in the cream, mace, and pepper and heat through for 2 minutes.
6. Add the shrimp and scallops and cook gently for 5 minutes.
7. Place the linguini in a warm serving dish. Top with the sauce and serve.

SEAFOOD AND SHELLS

PREPARATION TIME: 10 MINUTES   MARINATION TIME: 4 HOURS   YIELD: 4 SERVINGS

½ pound bay scallops, or deep sea scallops
    cut in quarters
⅓ cup fresh lemon juice (2 lemons)
8 ounces shell pasta
¾ pound medium-size shrimp, shelled and
    cleaned, or ½ pound shelled
    medium-size shrimp
¼ cup olive oil
½ cup vegetable oil
2 garlic cloves, crushed or minced
2 sprigs fresh dill, or ½–1 teaspoon dried dill
¼ teaspoon ground white pepper
½ cup ricotta
½ cup sour cream
⅛ teaspoon Tabasco sauce

1. Place the scallops in a large bowl with the lemon juice. Marinate for 4 hours in the refrigerator.
2. Cook the pasta according to the package directions. Then drain and rinse under cold water.
3. Drop the shrimp into a large pot of boiling water. As soon as they turn pink (1–2 minutes), remove and rinse under cold water.
4. Place the shrimp in the lemon juice with the scallops. Coat the shrimp and scallop pieces with the lemon juice.
5. Blend the oils, garlic, dill, pepper, ricotta, sour cream, and Tabasco.
6. Stir the ricotta mixture into the seafood and lemon juice (most of the lemon juice will be absorbed by this time). Add the shells and mix well. Refrigerate for several hours for the flavors to meld.

LINGUINI WITH RED CLAM SAUCE

PREPARATION TIME: 10 MINUTES   COOKING TIME: 30 MINUTES   YIELD: 4 SERVINGS

4 dozen littleneck clams, scrubbed
½ cup white wine
2 tablespoons olive oil
3 garlic cloves, crushed or minced
3 cups crushed tomatoes (1 28-ounce can)
1 teaspoon dried thyme
¼ teaspoon hot red pepper flakes
⅓ cup chopped parsley
1 pound thin linguini

1. Place the scrubbed clams in a pan with the wine and steam them until the shells open, about 10 minutes. Remove the clams from the shells and put them aside; reserve the broth.
2. Heat the oil in a skillet and sauté the garlic for 10 seconds.
3. Add 1 cup of the reserved clam broth, the tomatoes, thyme, pepper flakes, and parsley to the skillet. Simmer for 15 minutes uncovered.
4. While the sauce is thickening, cook the linguini according to the package directions. Drain and turn into a large, warm serving bowl.
5. Stir the cooked clams into the hot sauce, heat through, and pour the sauce over the pasta. Serve immediately.

WHITE CLAM SAUCE WITH THIN SPAGHETTI

PREPARATION TIME: 5 MINUTES   COOKING TIME: 10 MINUTES   YIELD: 2 SERVINGS

8 ounces thin spaghetti (capellini, perciatelle)
2 tablespoons butter
1 garlic clove, crushed or minced
2 tablespoons cornstarch
¼ cup white wine, clam juice, or chicken stock
1 10-ounce can whole baby clams in broth
1 6½-ounce can chopped clams
⅛ teaspoon ground white pepper
¼ cup chopped parsley

1. Cook the spaghetti in boiling water according to the package directions.
2. Melt the butter in a saucepan and sauté the garlic for 10 seconds.
3. Add the cornstarch and stir for 1 minute.
4. Pour in the white wine and the liquid from the cans of clams. Stir continuously until the sauce is smooth.
5. Add the clams, pepper, and parsley, and heat through for 5 minutes.
6. Drain the pasta and divide into two individual warm serving bowls. Top with the sauce and serve immediately.

CRAB ALLA ALFREDO

PREPARATION TIME: 5 MINUTES   COOKING TIME: 10 MINUTES   YIELD: 4 SIDE SERVINGS

1 pound shells, twists, or specialty shape
2 tablespoons butter
½ cup cream
1 tablespoon chopped shallots or chopped chives
⅛ teaspoon ground white pepper
½ pound chunk crab meat
¼ cup sour cream
¼ cup low-fat milk
¼ cup grated Parmesan cheese

There are many different stories of the derivation of the term "Alfredo." Alfredo was apparently a restaurateur whose name was given to one of his sauces. I have always considered Alfredo sauce to be a cream and butter sauce.

1. Cook the shells according to the package directions.
2. Put the butter, cream, shallots, and pepper in a saucepan and heat gently for 5 minutes. Remove from the heat.
3. Add the crab meat to the saucepan.
4. Stir the sour cream and milk together and blend into the crab mixture in the saucepan. Return to the heat and cook gently for 2 minutes.
5. Drain the shells and turn them into a warm serving dish. Add the crab mixture and stir in the grated Parmesan. Serve immediately.

CRAB, DILL, AND SHELL SALAD

PREPARATION TIME: 15 MINUTES   COOKING TIME: 10 MINUTES   YIELD: 4 SERVINGS

8 ounces shell pasta
½ cup mayonnaise
½ cup sour cream
1 tablespoon lemon juice
¼ teaspoon coarsely ground black pepper
1 tablespoon fresh chopped dill, or 1 teaspoon dried dill
1 pound crab or lobster meat

You can stretch this dish without robbing it of flavor by using 12 ounces of pasta instead of 8. In either case, be generous when you measure the mayonnaise and sour cream. I like to serve this salad with extra chopped fresh dill on the side.

1. Cook the shells according to the package directions. Drain and rinse under cold water.
2. Mix the mayonnaise, sour cream, lemon juice, pepper, and dill in a large serving bowl.
3. Stir in the crab and the cold shells.
4. Serve immediately or chill. If you chill the salad, allow it to sit at room temperature for 15–30 minutes before serving in order to bring out the delicate flavor of the crab.

STEAMED MUSSELS WITH LINGUINI

PREPARATION TIME: 15 MINUTES   COOKING TIME: 15 MINUTES   YIELD: 6 SERVINGS

4 pounds mussels, scrubbed and beards removed
½ cup white wine
½ cup cream or half-and-half
1 tablespoon dried thyme
1 tablespoon dried tarragon
2 garlic cloves, crushed or minced
1 pound thin linguini
¼ cup olive oil
1 medium-size onion, chopped
1 garlic clove, crushed or minced
1 red bell pepper, chopped
½ teaspoon coarsely ground black pepper
¼ cup chopped parsley
½ cup grated Parmesan cheese

1. Place the mussels in a large kettle. Mix the wine, cream, thyme, tarragon, and 2 garlic cloves. Pour this mixture over the mussels, cover the pan, and cook over medium heat for 5–10 minutes, until all the shells have opened.
2. Remove the mussels from the pot and reserve 1 cup of the broth. Remove the mussels from their shells as soon as they can be handled, and set them aside.
3. Cook the linguini in boiling water according to the package directions.
4. Heat the olive oil in a skillet and sauté the onion, garlic clove, and red pepper for 5–10 minutes. Remove from the heat and add the shelled mussels to the skillet.
5. Reheat the mussel broth.
6. Drain the linguini and place in a warm serving dish. Pour the hot broth over the linguini and toss in the pepper, parsley, and Parmesan. Top with the mussel mixture and serve immediately.

THE POWER OF PASTA

MUSSELS RÉMOULADE

½ pound penne or other cut, hollow macaroni
4 pounds mussels, scrubbed and beards removed
½ cup white wine or water
½ cup mayonnaise
½ cup plain yogurt
3 tablespoons mild Dijon mustard
1 teaspoon dried tarragon, or 2 tablespoons
    chopped, fresh tarragon
2 teaspoons dried oregano, or 2 tablespoons
    chopped, fresh oregano
1 tablespoon capers, chopped
2 tablespoons lemon juice, white wine, or
    pickle juice
¼ teaspoon coarsely ground black pepper

The so-called "beards" on mussels are the whiskers poking out of one end of the shell. I usually just scrub them off as I clean the mussels.

1. Cook the penne in boiling water according to the package directions. Drain and rinse in cold water.
2. Steam the mussels in ½ cup wine for 5–10 minutes, until all the shells have opened. Remove the mussels from the shells and set them aside. Discard the liquid.
3. Combine the rest of the ingredients in a large serving bowl. Add the mussels and the cooked pasta. Mix and chill.

SMOKED SALMON WITH FETTUCCINE

PREPARATION TIME: 5 MINUTES   COOKING TIME: 10 MINUTES   YIELD: 2 SERVINGS

8 ounces fettuccine noodles
½ cup cream or half-and-half
1 garlic clove, crushed or minced
⅛ teaspoon ground white pepper
1 teaspoon dried dill, or 2 tablespoons
　　chopped, fresh dill
1 teaspoon mild prepared mustard
½ cup sour cream
¼ pound smoked salmon, cut in small pieces
¼ cup grated Parmesan cheese

1. Cook the fettuccine in boiling water according to the package directions.
2. Heat the cream, garlic, pepper, dill, and mustard in a small saucepan.
3. Stir in the sour cream and the smoked salmon.
4. Drain the fettuccine and place in a warm serving dish. Top with the sauce and the Parmesan cheese. Serve immediately.

ORIENTAL PASTA

It's not a great insight to remark upon the obvious association between pasta and Italian cooking. And it's true that most of the recipes in this cookbook originate in the Italian cuisine — but not all of them. A few recipes, such as Kreplach (page 44) and Spaetzle (page 43), indicate by their names that they come from other cultures. However, in our exploration of the joys of pasta, I believe that the Orient deserves a bit of special attention.

While we may not think of egg rolls and won tons as pasta dishes, that's exactly what they are — and truly wonderful ones at that. The noodles speak for themselves.

ANN KOJIS'S COLD SPICY SZECHUAN NOODLES

PREPARATION TIME: 10 MINUTES   COOKING TIME: 10 MINUTES   YIELD: 6–8 SIDE SERVINGS

1 pound Chinese noodles or thin linguini
6 tablespoons soy sauce
2 tablespoons hot chili oil
⅓ cup water or chicken stock
¼ cup peanut oil
½ cup sesame paste
2 tablespoons sesame oil
2 tablespoons rice vinegar
2 teaspoons sugar
12–16 garlic cloves, minced
½ cup toasted sesame seeds
10 scallions, sliced thin

This sauce has a powerful kick to it and will appeal to garlic and hot sauce lovers. The first time I made it I automatically cut the hot chili oil and garlic quantities in half. The second time I used only 4 large cloves of garlic and that turned out to be just my speed.

Hot chili oil is frequently used in Szechuan cooking. It can be found where Chinese food is sold.

1. Cook the noodles according to the package directions, drain, and rinse under cold water.
2. Place the rest of the ingredients, except the sesame seeds and scallions, in a blender, food processor, or mixing bowl. Blend well.
3. Add the sesame seeds to the sauce and pour over the cold noodles.
4. Sprinkle with the scallions and serve immediately or refrigerate.

CHICKEN STIR-FRY WITH NOODLES

PREPARATION TIME: 15 MINUTES   COOKING TIME: 10 MINUTES   YIELD: 4 SERVINGS

½ pound Oriental noodles
3 quarts water
1 tablespoon sesame oil or peanut oil
2 teaspoons cornstarch
1 tablespoon soy sauce
1 tablespoon rice wine or dry sherry
1 tablespoon peanut oil
1 whole chicken breast, boned, sliced,
    and cut in 1-inch pieces
1 tablespoon peanut oil
1 medium-size green bell pepper, chopped
4 scallions, thinly sliced
1 large garlic clove, crushed or minced
1 inch fresh ginger root, peeled and minced
1 small (6-inch) zucchini, sliced and julienned
1 cup chicken stock

1. Cook the noodles in 3 quarts of boiling water for approximately 2 minutes. Drain and toss with the sesame oil.
2. Make a marinade of the cornstarch, soy sauce, rice wine, and 1 tablespoon peanut oil. Add the chicken pieces. Turn to coat.
3. Heat 1 tablespoon peanut oil in a wok or large skillet and add the green pepper. Stir-fry for 2 minutes over medium-high heat.
4. Add the scallions, garlic, and ginger root and stir-fry for 1 minute.
5. Remove the chicken pieces from the marinade with a slotted spoon and add them to the wok. Stir-fry for 2 minutes.
6. Add the marinade and the zucchini. Mix with a wooden spatula and stir-fry for 2 minutes.
7. Stir in the stock and the noodles and cook for 3 minutes. Serve immediately.

TOFU EGG ROLLS

PREPARATION TIME: 30 MINUTES   COOKING TIME: 30 MINUTES   YIELD: 4–6 SERVINGS (12 EGG ROLLS)

2 tablespoons vegetable oil
2 garlic cloves, crushed or minced
1 teaspoon chopped fresh ginger root
¼ pound mushrooms, chopped
¼ cup thinly sliced scallion greens
½ pound tofu, diced fine
½ cup bean sprouts
1 tablespoon soy sauce
1 tablespoon sesame oil
12 egg roll wrappers — approximately 6 x 6 inches
4–6 tablespoons vegetable oil

1. Heat the 2 tablespoons of oil in a skillet and sauté the garlic, ginger, mushrooms, and scallion greens for 2 minutes.
2. Add the tofu, bean sprouts, soy sauce, and sesame oil and heat gently for about 5 minutes.
3. Remove to a dish and cool for 5 minutes.
4. Place 3–4 tablespoons of the mixture on each wrapper just above center. Fold the *corner* nearest you over the filling. Fold in the two sides and roll down to the bottom corner. Brush the corner edge with a little water and seal.
5. Continue in this way until all 12 wrappers have been filled and rolled.
6. Heat 4–6 tablespoons of oil in a skillet and fry 3–4 egg rolls at a time, until they are golden brown, about 5 minutes.
7. Serve with Spicy Sauce (page 97).

ORIENTAL PASTA

FRIED WON TONS WITH SPICY SAUCE

PREPARATION TIME: 1 HOUR   COOKING TIME: 5–10 MINUTES   YIELD: 4–6 SERVINGS (40 WON TONS)

1 pound ground pork
2 tablespoons soy sauce
2 tablespoons sesame oil
2 garlic cloves, crushed or minced
6 scallions, sliced very fine
40 won ton skins — approximately 2 x 3 inches
2–6 tablespoons vegetable oil

1. Combine the pork, soy sauce, sesame oil, garlic, and scallions in a bowl.
2. Stuff each won ton skin with 1½–2 teaspoons of the mixture. Fold the skin in half, dampen the edges with a little water, and pinch all around to seal. (Keep the rest of the won ton skins covered with a damp cloth to prevent them from drying out.)
3. Pour 2 tablespoons of oil in a skillet and heat. Fry a small quantity of won tons at a time for about 2 minutes on each side, then on the bottom until it becomes a little brown — about 3 minutes. Repeat until all the won tons have been fried. Add more oil to the pan as needed.
4. Return all won tons to the skillet. Pour in a little water, cover the skillet, and cook for 5 minutes, until all the liquid has evaporated.
5. Serve with Spicy Sauce.

Variation

If boiled won tons are preferred, bring 4 quarts of water to a boil and drop about 10 won tons at a time into the pot. Boil for about 5 minutes. Remove with a slotted spoon. Serve with Spicy Sauce or floating in hot beef broth.

SPICY SAUCE

1 tablespoon prepared mustard
¼ cup soy sauce
¼ cup chicken broth
2 tablespoons sesame oil
1 tablespoon mild vinegar
½ teaspoon sugar
1 teaspoon minced fresh ginger root
2 tablespoons sliced scallion greens
1 teaspoon hot sesame oil or hot chili oil

1. Mix all the ingredients in a small bowl.
2. Serve in small individual dishes. Dip the won tons into the sauce.

MARINATED CHICKEN WITH SESAME NOODLES

PREPARATION TIME: 20 MINUTES   MARINATION TIME: 4 HOURS   COOKING TIME: 45 MINUTES
YIELD: 4 SERVINGS

½ cup sesame seed paste
1½ cups plain yogurt
½ cup white wine
½ cup peanut oil
½ cup soy sauce
1 tablespoon hot sesame oil (optional)
2–4 garlic cloves
1 teaspoon ground ginger, or 1-inch peeled, fresh ginger root, chopped
1 pound Chinese noodles or thin spaghetti, cooked according to the package directions and rinsed immediately in cold water
½ cup sliced scallion greens or chopped fresh chives
1 4–5-pound chicken, cut into breasts, wings, thighs, and drumsticks

Middle Eastern tahini is a sweeter sesame seed paste than the dark Oriental pastes.

1. Place all the ingredients, except the noodles, the scallion greens, and the chicken, in a blender and blend until smooth.
2. Toss 1½ cups of sauce with the cold, cooked noodles. Turn into a serving bowl, sprinkle with the scallion greens, cover, and refrigerate.
3. Place the chicken pieces in a shallow baking dish and cover with the remaining sauce. Coat each piece. Cover the dish, and refrigerate for 4 hours or longer.
4. Barbecue the chicken 6 inches from the heat, over grey coals. Cover the barbecue and cook for 45 minutes, turning the pieces every 15 minutes.
5. Remove the noodles from the refrigerator half an hour before the chicken is done. Serve with the barbecued chicken.

Variation

In place of barbecuing, bake the chicken in a 400° F. oven for 55 minutes. Keep covered with aluminum foil for the first 30 minutes.

GINGER NOODLES WITH FLANK STEAK

PREPARATION TIME: 15 MINUTES   COOKING TIME: 15 MINUTES   YIELD: 4 SERVINGS

2 teaspoons ground ginger, or 2 inches peeled,
   fresh ginger root, minced
2 tablespoons soy sauce
2 tablespoons sesame paste (tahini)
1 teaspoon hot chili oil
1½ cups chicken stock
4 scallions, thinly sliced
1 pound flank steak
1 pound Oriental noodles or capellini

1. Blend together the ginger, soy sauce, sesame paste, hot oil, and stock. Stir in the scallions.
2. Pour ½ cup of this mixture over the flank steak and marinate for 15 minutes, turning after 7–8 minutes.
3. Cook the noodles according to the package directions. Drain, rinse under cold water, and place in a large, long serving dish with the remaining ginger sauce (about 1¼ cups).
4. Broil the flank steak close to the heat, 4 minutes a side for rare meat. Slice across the grain (the width) into thin strips, and cut in half so that each piece is about 2 inches long. Toss the steak in the marinade and arrange it on top of the noodles. Serve immediately or chill.

ORIENTAL PASTA

PASTA SALADS

This is the chapter to turn to when you arrive home late and tired. Each recipe provides a complete balance of protein and complex carbohydrates and can be prepared in 10 to 15 minutes. I love to prepare pasta salads for summer eating — whether for two or ten people. In fact, a menu of two or three different salads can make entertaining an easy and truly enjoyable affair. Make them a day ahead, if possible, so the flavors can meld, and take them out of the refrigerator about a half hour before you're ready to serve. Place them on the serving table and enjoy the party.

While the salads in this chapter represent a wide range of possibilities, there are more cold pasta recipes tucked into the Pasta and Seafood and the Oriental Pasta chapters. Don't overlook the delicate Crab, Dill, and Shell Salad (page 87), the Mussels Rémoulade (page 89), or Ann Kojis's Spicy Szechuan Noodles (page 93).

SHELLS WITH AVOCADO SAUCE

PREPARATION TIME: 10 MINUTES   COOKING TIME: 10 MINUTES   YIELD: 4–6 SERVINGS

1 pound small shells
2 cups mashed ripe avocado (2 medium-size
    or 1 very large avocado)
1 tablespoon lemon juice
½ cup sour cream
½ cup mayonnaise
½ cup "medium" or "mild" vegetable taco sauce
½ cup sliced scallions
1 garlic clove, crushed or minced
½ teaspoon cumin powder

1. Cook the shells in boiling water according to the package directions. Drain and rinse under cold water. Place in a large serving bowl.
2. Beat the rest of the ingredients together until smooth. Combine with the shells. Serve immediately or chill.

MOZZARELLA, BASIL, AND TOMATO PASTA SALAD

PREPARATION TIME: 10 MINUTES   COOKING TIME: 10 MINUTES   YIELD: 4 SIDE SERVINGS

8 ounces elbow macaroni, penne, or cut ziti
8 ounces low-fat mozzarella, sliced thin and
    cut in bite-size pieces
1 cup basil leaves
2 cups cherry tomatoes, cut in half
¼ cup olive oil
¾ cup vegetable oil
2 tablespoons lemon juice
1 teaspoon dried oregano
1–2 garlic cloves, crushed or minced

1. Cook the macaroni according to the package directions.
2. Place the rest of the ingredients in a large serving bowl and mix.
3. Drain the macaroni and add to the mozzarella mixture. Toss to combine and serve immediately.

JIM BRADY'S ORZO SALAD

PREPARATION TIME: 20 MINUTES   COOKING TIME: 10 MINUTES   YIELD: 8–10 SIDE SERVINGS

1 pound orzo pasta
1 bay leaf
½ cup olive oil
½ cup fresh lemon juice
2 garlic cloves, crushed or minced
½ teaspoon coarsely ground black pepper
½ cup chopped parsley
½ cup cubed feta cheese
½ cup diced tomatoes or cherry tomatoes
    cut in half
½ cup halved pitted olives
½–1 cup any combination of fresh garden
    vegetables, cut in bite-size pieces (broccoli,
    green beans, green pepper, red pepper,
    zucchini, carrots)

1. Cook the orzo with the bay leaf according to the package directions. Drain and rinse under cold water.
2. Combine the oil, lemon juice, garlic, pepper, and parsley in a jar with a tight lid and shake to blend.
3. Place the rest of the ingredients in a large serving bowl and toss with the pasta and the oil dressing. Chill before serving.

MUSHROOM AND MACARONI SALAD

PREPARATION TIME: 10 MINUTES   COOKING TIME: 10 MINUTES   YIELD: 6 SIDE SERVINGS

12 ounces hollow, cut macaroni
1 pound mushrooms, sliced (4 cups)
1 pound fresh tomatoes (4 medium-size
   tomatoes), cut in bite-size pieces
1 large carrot, grated (1 cup)
¼ cup chopped parsley
½ cup grated Romano cheese
¾ cup vegetable oil
¼ cup olive oil
¼ cup wine vinegar
3 garlic cloves, crushed or minced
½ teaspoon coarsely ground black pepper
1½ teaspoons dried thyme
2–3 large shallots, chopped fine

1. Cook the macaroni according to the package directions. Drain and rinse under cold water. Place in a large serving bowl.
2. Add the mushrooms, tomatoes, carrot, parsley, and cheese to the bowl.
3. Combine the remaining ingredients in a jar with a tight lid and shake to blend. Pour over the vegetables and macaroni and toss together. Chill for several hours, if desired.

CURRIED LENTILS AND DITALINI

PREPARATION TIME: 15 MINUTES   COOKING TIME: 1 HOUR   YIELD: 4–6 SERVINGS

1 pound lentils, cooked 1 hour in 6 cups water,
    or 4½ cups cooked lentils
1 cup ditalini, cooked according to package
    directions, drained, and rinsed under cold
    water, or 2 cups cooked small macaroni
½ cup finely chopped celery
½ cup finely sliced scallions
½ cup chopped parsley
1⅓ cups vegetable oil
⅓ cup fresh lemon juice
3 garlic cloves, crushed or minced
1 tablespoon curry powder

*This dish gets better as it matures. Make it a
day ahead if possible.*

1. Place the cooked lentils, macaroni, celery,
   scallions, and parsley in a large serving bowl.
2. Measure the oil, lemon juice, garlic, and curry
   powder into a jar with a tight lid and shake vig-
   orously to blend. Pour over the lentil mixture
   and toss together. Serve immediately or chill.

WHITE KIDNEY BEANS AND SCALLIONS

PREPARATION TIME: 10 MINUTES   COOKING TIME: 10 MINUTES   YIELD: 4 SERVINGS

12 ounces shells or hollow macaroni
½ cup olive oil
2 tablespoons lemon juice
1½ teaspoons dried oregano
1 teaspoon dried thyme
2–4 garlic cloves, crushed or minced
1 16-ounce can white kidney beans
   (cannelini) with liquid
1 cup sliced scallions (about 8 large scallions,
   including green)
1 cup cherry tomatoes, cut in half
1 cup sliced mushrooms
2 hard-boiled eggs, diced (optional)

1. Cook the pasta according to the package directions.
2. Mix the oil, lemon juice, oregano, thyme, garlic, and cannelini in a large serving bowl.
3. Stir in the scallions, tomatoes, mushrooms, and eggs.
4. Drain the pasta and toss with the rest of the ingredients. Serve immediately or chill.

CHICKEN CURRY MACARONI

PREPARATION TIME: 10 MINUTES   COOKING TIME: 10 MINUTES   YIELD: 6–8 SERVINGS

1½ pounds rotelle (twists)
4 cups cubed cooked chicken
1 large garlic clove, crushed or minced
2 teaspoons curry powder
¼ teaspoon ground black pepper
1 large egg, beaten
1 tablespoon honey
3 tablespoons lemon juice
1 tablespoon dried thyme, or ¼ cup fresh
   lemon thyme leaves
½ cup sour cream
¼ cup olive oil
¾ cup vegetable oil
1 cup chopped parsley
1 cup chopped chives or scallion greens

1. Cook the rotelle in boiling water according to the package directions. Drain and rinse under cold water.
2. Place in a large serving dish with the cubed chicken.
3. Blend the garlic, curry powder, pepper, egg, honey, lemon juice, thyme, and sour cream. Add the oils in one continuous thin stream, stirring constantly, until the mixture is thick and smooth.
4. Stir in the parsley and chives.
5. Pour over the chicken and pasta and combine thoroughly. Serve immediately or chill.

MACARONI AND THREE-BEAN SALAD

PREPARATION TIME: 10 MINUTES   COOKING TIME: 10 MINUTES   YIELD: 4 SERVINGS

12 ounces cut ziti or elbow macaroni
1 16-ounce can red kidney beans with liquid
1 16-ounce can lima beans with liquid
1 cup fresh runner beans, sliced, or frozen cut
    green beans, steamed for 5 minutes
4 large scallions, sliced (½ cup)
1 garlic clove, crushed or minced
1 tablespoon dried oregano
½ teaspoon paprika
1 teaspoon powdered mustard, or 1
    tablespoon prepared mustard
⅔ cup vegetable oil
⅓ cup olive oil
¼ cup lemon juice
¼ teaspoon coarsely ground black pepper
¼ cup grated Romano cheese

1. Cook the pasta in boiling water according to the package directions. Drain and rinse under cold water. Place in a large serving bowl.
2. Add the canned beans (plus liquids), cooked fresh beans, and scallions.
3. Place all the remaining ingredients in a jar with a tight lid and shake to blend. Pour the dressing over the pasta and beans, toss together, and chill for several hours to enhance the flavors.

CAROL HARCARIK'S PASTA PRIMAVERA SALAD

PREPARATION TIME: 15 MINUTES   COOKING TIME: 10 MINUTES   YIELD: 4 SIDE SERVINGS

8 ounces cut ziti
1 cup broccoli florets
1 cup sliced carrots
1 small zucchini, sliced
1 cup tiny frozen peas
1 cup cut green beans
½ cup pitted black olives
3 scallions, sliced
6 radishes, cut in half
1 small green bell pepper, chopped
1 slice pimento, chopped
½ cup red wine
½ cup olive oil or peanut oil
½ cup mayonnaise
salt and pepper to taste
¼ cup chopped parsley

If my neighbor Carol Harcarik is really rushed for time, she throws a package of mixed frozen vegetables in with the pasta 5 minutes before it finishes cooking.

1. Bring a 3–4-quart pot of water to a boil and throw in the ziti.
2. Five minutes before it finishes cooking, add the broccoli, carrots, zucchini, peas, and green beans to the pasta.
3. Drain and rinse immediately under cold water.
4. Place in a large serving bowl with the olives, scallions, radishes, bell pepper, and pimento.
5. In a small bowl, combine the red wine, oil, mayonnaise, salt and pepper, and parsley. Pour over the vegetables and pasta and combine thoroughly. Serve immediately or chill until later.

TUNA AND OLIVE SALAD

PREPARATION TIME: 15 MINUTES   COOKING TIME: 10 MINUTES   YIELD: 4 SERVINGS

¾ pound cut, hollow macaroni
12 ounces mushrooms, sliced
1 cup pitted black olives, sliced
6 large scallions, sliced
2 6½-ounce cans solid white tuna in water,
    drained and flaked
½ cup chopped parsley
¼ cup white wine
¼ cup lemon juice
⅓ cup olive oil
1 cup vegetable oil
1 tablespoon mild prepared mustard
2 teaspoons dried oregano
2 teaspoons dried thyme
2 large garlic cloves, crushed or minced

1. Cook the macaroni according to the package directions. Then drain and rinse under cold water.
2. Place the macaroni, mushrooms, olives, scallions, tuna, and parsley in a large serving bowl. Toss to combine.
3. Put the rest of the ingredients in a jar with a tight lid and shake to blend. Pour over the macaroni mixture and stir gently.
4. Refrigerate until ready to serve.

PASTA AND VEGETABLES

Vegetable recipes rate high in my book because they can be completely spontaneous. When I have nothing planned for dinner, or if the cupboard is bare, I clean out the vegetable drawer. As long as I have onions, garlic, a rib of celery, a carrot or two, or maybe an odd zucchini or a bell pepper that's seen better days, then I know that dinner is forthcoming. (Naturally, I depend on the fact that I have a large can of plum tomatoes in the bare cupboard next to the pasta.)

Let the recipes in this chapter spark your imagination — there is almost no limit to the number of variations you can create.

ZUCCHINI, MOZZARELLA, AND FUSILLI

PREPARATION TIME: 20 MINUTES   COOKING TIME: 10 MINUTES   YIELD: 4 SERVINGS

12 ounces long fusilli
¼ cup olive oil
2 tablespoons vegetable oil
1 large onion, chopped (2 cups)
2 red bell peppers, chopped (2 cups)
2 medium-size (6–7-inch) zucchini, chopped
   (2 cups)
2 teaspoons dried oregano
1 teaspoon dried thyme
¼ teaspoon coarsely ground black pepper
8 ounces mozzarella, grated (2 cups)
¼ cup chopped parsley
½ cup grated Parmesan or Romano cheese

1. Cook the fusilli in boiling water, according to the package directions.
2. Heat the oils in a large skillet and sauté the onion, bell peppers, zucchini, oregano, thyme, and pepper for 10 minutes.
3. Combine the mozzarella, parsley, and Parmesan and toss with the drained, hot pasta.
4. Turn the pasta onto a warm serving dish and top with the sautéed vegetables. Serve immediately or toss the vegetables into the pasta and serve or chill.

CARROT AND ASPARAGUS SPAGHETTI

PREPARATION TIME: 10 MINUTES   COOKING TIME: 10 MINUTES   YIELD: 4 SIDE SERVINGS

8 ounces very thin spaghetti
8 ounces carrots, sliced very thin (1½ cups)
8 ounces asparagus, stems peeled and cut in
   1-inch pieces (1½ cups)
1 tablespoon olive oil
2 tablespoons butter
1 very small garlic clove, crushed or minced
½ teaspoon coarsely ground black pepper
¼ cup chopped parsley
⅓ cup sour cream
2 tablespoons low-fat milk
⅓ cup grated Parmesan cheese

1. Cook the spaghetti in boiling water according to the package directions.
2. Steam the carrots and asparagus for 5 minutes.
3. Heat the olive oil and butter in a skillet and sauté the garlic for 10 seconds. Add the drained vegetable pieces, pepper, and parsley. Sauté for 1 minute.
4. Beat together the sour cream and milk. Add to the skillet, stir, and heat through gently for about 2 minutes.
5. Drain the spaghetti and toss with the sauce and Parmesan cheese. Serve immediately.

THE POWER OF PASTA

MUSHROOM-BROCCOLI SHELLS

PREPARATION TIME: 15 MINUTES   COOKING TIME: 10 MINUTES   YIELD: 4–6 SIDE SERVINGS

8 ounces macaroni shells
2 broccoli heads, cut into florets and stem
**   pieces (about 1 pound)**
¼ cup olive oil
2 garlic cloves, crushed or minced
8 ounces mushrooms, sliced
1 8-ounce can tomato sauce
¼ cup cream
¼ teaspoon coarsely ground black pepper
1 teaspoon dried oregano
¼ cup grated Romano cheese

1. Cook the shells in boiling water according to the package directions.
2. Steam the broccoli pieces for 5 minutes. Drain off the water and keep the broccoli covered in the pan.
3. Heat the oil in a skillet and sauté the garlic for 10 seconds. Add the mushroom slices and stir-fry for 1 minute over medium heat.
4. Add the tomato sauce, cream, pepper, and oregano to the skillet. Bring to a boil and turn off the heat.
5. Stir the broccoli pieces into the sauce.
6. Drain the shells and add them to the sauce.
7. Sprinkle with the grated Romano and serve immediately.

BROCCOLI TWIST

PREPARATION TIME: 10 MINUTES   COOKING TIME: 15 MINUTES   YIELD: 4–6 SIDE SERVINGS

2 broccoli heads, cut into bite-size florets and
  stem pieces
½ pound twists (rotelle or cut fusilli)
2 tablespoons olive oil
6 scallions, sliced thin
2 garlic cloves, crushed or minced
¼ teaspoon coarsely ground black pepper
¼ cup cream
¼ cup grated Parmesan cheese

I like to serve this dish with ham or poultry.

1. Steam the broccoli for 8 minutes, until al dente crunchy. Pour off the water and return the broccoli to the pan. Keep it covered.
2. Cook the twists in boiling water according to the package directions.
3. Heat the olive oil in a skillet over medium heat and sauté the scallions, garlic, and pepper for 30 seconds.
4. Add the cream to the scallions and garlic. Then add the broccoli pieces, and heat gently for 1 minute.
5. Drain the twists, return them to their pan, and stir in the heated broccoli and scallions.
6. Sprinkle with Parmesan cheese and toss together. Serve immediately.

Variation

This dish is also excellent when baked. Turn the broccoli-twist combination into a lightly greased baking dish. Pour ½ cup tomato juice and ½ cup cream over the casserole. Sprinkle with 2 tablespoons of grated Parmesan and bake in a preheated oven at 400° F. for 15–20 minutes.

TOMATO-SPINACH PASTA FRITTATA

PREPARATION TIME: 10 MINUTES   COOKING TIME: 15 MINUTES   YIELD: 2 SERVINGS

2 medium-size fresh tomatoes, cut in thin wedges
1 cup fresh spinach leaves, or ½ cup frozen,
    thawed and drained
1 tablespoon vegetable oil
1 cup leftover cooked pasta (with or
    without dressing)
4 large eggs, beaten
2 tablespoons water
½ teaspoon coarsely ground black pepper
½ cup grated Parmesan or Romano cheese

1. In a skillet, sauté the tomatoes and spinach in oil for 2 minutes over medium heat.
2. Add the pasta to the vegetables and cook for 8 minutes.
3. Mix the eggs, water, pepper, and Parmesan and pour over the pasta and vegetables. Cover and cook for 5 minutes, until the eggs set. Slide onto a warm serving plate and serve.

PASTA WITH MUSHROOMS AND WINE

PREPARATION TIME: 15 MINUTES   COOKING TIME: 30 MINUTES   YIELD: 4–6 SERVINGS

2 tablespoons butter
3 tablespoons olive oil or vegetable oil
1½ pounds mushrooms, sliced
¼ cup chopped parsley
4 garlic cloves, crushed or minced
½ cup white wine or chicken broth
½ teaspoon coarsely ground black pepper
1 pound thin spaghetti or capellini
1 tablespoon olive oil or butter
½ cup grated Parmesan cheese

1. Heat the butter and oil in a large skillet and sauté the mushrooms, parsley, and garlic for 5 minutes, stirring frequently.
2. Add the wine or broth and black pepper. Simmer for 20 minutes.
3. Cook the pasta according to the package directions. Drain and toss with the tablespoon of oil or butter and the Parmesan. Top with the mushroom sauce. Serve immediately.

CAVATELLI PRIMAVERA

8 ounces cavatelli, shells, or twists
1 medium-size (7-inch) carrot, sliced
½ cauliflower head, cut into bite-size pieces
   (2 cups)
1 10-ounce package frozen tiny tender peas
1 medium-size (7-inch) zucchini, sliced
1 large red bell pepper, cut into bite-size pieces
½ cup milk or cream, scalded
1 egg, beaten
2 tablespoons white wine
⅓ cup olive oil
2 garlic cloves, crushed or minced
¼ teaspoon coarsely ground black pepper
¼ cup chopped parsley

This dish is delicious served warm or chilled.

1. Bring water to boil in a 5-quart pot. Cook the pasta according to the package directions.
2. Five minutes before the end of cooking, add the carrot, cauliflower, and frozen peas to the pasta. After 3 more minutes add the zucchini and bell pepper. Cook for 2 minutes. Drain pasta and vegetables immediately.
3. Beat the remaining ingredients together and pour the sauce over the pasta and vegetables. Toss together gently. Serve immediately.

PROSCIUTTO-MOZZARELLA WITH SWEET RED PEPPERS

PREPARATION TIME: 10 MINUTES   COOKING TIME: 10 MINUTES   YIELD: 4 SERVINGS

2 large sweet red bell peppers
12 ounces linguini or spaghetti
8 ounces rolled prosciutto and mozzarella, diced
¼ cup olive oil
¼ cup vegetable oil
2–4 garlic cloves, crushed or minced
¼ teaspoon coarsely ground black pepper
½ teaspoon hot red pepper flakes
½ cup chopped parsley
½ cup grated Parmesan or Romano cheese

I like to blanch the red bell peppers and slip off the skins. It's certainly not necessary, but I think it enhances the texture and complements the prosciutto-mozzarella even better. You should be able to find mozzarella stuffed with prosciutto at the supermarket.

1. Remove the stem and seeds from the bell peppers and drop the peppers into 4 quarts boiling water. Blanch for 2 minutes, remove, slip off the skins, and dice the peppers.
2. Drop the linguini into the same boiling water and cook according to the package directions.
3. Place the diced peppers, diced prosciutto and mozzarella, oils, garlic, black pepper, and hot pepper flakes into a large serving bowl.
4. Drain the cooked pasta, toss with the prosciutto-mozzarella mixture, and gently mix in the chopped parsley and grated Parmesan. Serve immediately in warm dishes.

SIMPLE GARLIC-AND-MUSHROOM PASTA

PREPARATION TIME: 5 MINUTES   COOKING TIME: 10 MINUTES   YIELD: 4 SIDE SERVINGS

8 ounces thin spaghetti or linguini
¼ cup olive oil
1 pound mushrooms, thinly sliced
2–4 garlic cloves, crushed or minced
½ teaspoon coarsely ground black pepper
¼ cup grated Parmesan or Romano cheese

1. Cook the spaghetti according to the package directions.
2. When the spaghetti has been boiling for 4 minutes, heat the olive oil in a large skillet.
3. Add the mushroom slices, garlic, and pepper to the skillet and sauté for 3 minutes, stirring constantly.
4. Drain the pasta and place in a large warmed serving bowl. Toss with the cooked mushrooms and garlic and sprinkle with the grated cheese. Serve immediately.

THE POWER OF PASTA

SPECIAL
SAUCES

The starchy blandness of macaroni is a perfect foil for a wide variety of sauces. Chunky beef, chicken, and thick red tomato sauces may be teamed with hollow pastas, smooth or grooved, short or long, and also the longer linguini and spaghetti. Linguini, spaghettini, angel hair, and fettuccine pastas are ideal for simple oil and grated cheese combinations, herb butters, and creamy, seafood, and no-cook sauces. The simplest sauce, concocted of odds and ends from the vegetable drawer, can turn a dish of pasta into a healthful and delectable meal that costs but nickels and dimes — a fact with most pasta sauces.

For most cooked sauces, I prefer to use canned, imported plum tomatoes. The consistency is thicker and the flavor fuller than even fresh tomatoes for the simple reason that only the ripest tomatoes are canned. The tomatoes I buy from local stores are often not worth the bother. They are not fully ripe (they are usually hard), they are watery, and they have no flavor. The only fresh tomatoes that I use are vine ripened from farmers' markets or my own garden.

TOMATO SAUCE I

PREPARATION TIME: 2 MINUTES   COOKING TIME: 10 MINUTES   YIELD: 3 CUPS

1 28-ounce can tomato sauce, purée, or crushed
   tomatoes (3 cups)
6 scallions, thinly sliced
1 teaspoon dried oregano
1 teaspoon dried basil
1 bay leaf

1. Place all the ingredients in a skillet over medium heat and cook for 5 minutes.
2. Reduce the heat and simmer for another 5 minutes. Serve immediately over hot pasta.

TOMATO SAUCE II

PREPARATION TIME: 10 MINUTES   COOKING TIME: 30 MINUTES   YIELD: 5½ CUPS

1 tablespoon olive oil or vegetable oil
1 medium-size onion, processed fine or grated
1 garlic clove, crushed or minced
3 pounds ripe tomatoes, roughly chopped
   (10 tomatoes)
½ cup fresh basil leaves
¼ teaspoon coarsely ground black pepper

1. Heat the oil in a skillet over medium heat. Add the onion and garlic and sauté for 5 minutes.
2. Add the tomatoes, basil leaves, and pepper. Cover the pan and simmer over low heat for 25 minutes.
3. Spoon half of the mixture into a blender or food processor and purée. Repeat with the remaining half.
4. Combine the two halves of the sauce and serve at once over hot pasta, or freeze one half for later use.

ZUCCHINI-TOMATO SAUCE

PREPARATION TIME: 10 MINUTES   COOKING TIME: 30 MINUTES   YIELD: 6 CUPS

1 tablespoon olive oil or vegetable oil
1 medium-size onion, chopped fine
2 garlic cloves, crushed or minced
3 cups tomatoes, chopped (fresh cooked or canned crushed)
1 tablespoon dried oregano
½ teaspoon coarsely ground black pepper
1 pound zucchini, chopped (4 6-inch zucchini)

1. Heat the oil in a skillet over medium heat. Add the onion and garlic and sauté for 5 minutes.
2. Add the tomatoes, oregano, and pepper and simmer for 15 minutes.
3. Add the chopped zucchini and cook 10 minutes more.
4. Spoon half the mixture into a blender or food processor and purée. Repeat with the remaining half.
5. Combine the two halves of the sauce and serve at once over hot pasta, or freeze one half for later use.

CURRIED TOFU SAUCE

PREPARATION TIME: 15 MINUTES   COOKING TIME: 30 MINUTES   YIELD: 6 CUPS

2 tablespoons olive oil
2 cups chopped onion (1 large onion)
1 cup chopped carrot (1 large carrot)
1 cup chopped celery (2 6-inch ribs)
2 garlic cloves, crushed or minced
2 teaspoons curry powder
1 28-ounce can crushed tomatoes
½ pound tofu, diced small

1. Heat the oil in a large skillet and sauté the onion, carrot, celery, garlic, and curry powder for 10 minutes, stirring occasionally.
2. Add the crushed tomatoes and diced tofu, stir together, and cook for 20 minutes over a gentle heat. Serve over hot pasta.

MUSHROOM-AND-WALNUT TOMATO SAUCE

PREPARATION TIME: 5 MINUTES   COOKING TIME: 10 MINUTES   YIELD: 2½ CUPS

2 tablespoons olive oil
2 large garlic cloves, crushed or minced
4 scallions, including green tops, sliced
8 ounces mushrooms, sliced
¼ cup chopped walnuts
1 cup tomato sauce
1 cup canned crushed tomatoes
1 tablespoon dried basil
¼ teaspoon coarsely ground black pepper

1. Heat the olive oil in a skillet over medium heat and sauté the garlic and scallions for 30 seconds.
2. Add the sliced mushrooms and stir-fry for 1 minute.
3. Stir in the chopped walnuts and cook for 1 minute.
4. Add the tomato sauce, crushed tomatoes, basil, and pepper. Cook for 5–10 minutes. Serve immediately over hot pasta.

SHRIMP SAUCE

PREPARATION TIME: 5 MINUTES   COOKING TIME: 5 MINUTES   YIELD: 1 CUP

2 tablespoons olive oil
2 shallots, chopped
½ pound medium-size shrimp (12 shrimp),
    shelled and cut in ¼-inch pieces
½ cup cream
2 tablespoons butter
⅛ teaspoon ground white pepper

1. Heat the oil in a skillet and sauté the shallots and shrimp pieces for 1 minute.
2. Add the cream, butter, and pepper. Heat for 1 minute. Serve over hot pasta.

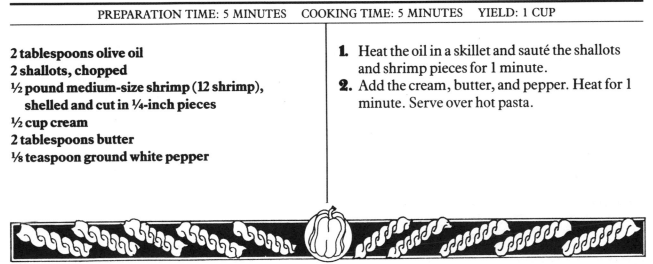

VEGETABLE SAUCE

PREPARATION TIME: 15 MINUTES   COOKING TIME: 35 MINUTES   YIELD: 3 QUARTS

¼ cup olive oil
2 medium-size onions, chopped (3 cups)
4 large carrots, thinly sliced (3 cups)
4 green or red bell peppers, chopped (3 cups)
6 garlic cloves, crushed or minced
2 medium-size zucchini, sliced and
    julienned (2 cups)
8 ounces mushrooms, sliced (2 cups)
6 cups tomato sauce
½ cup red wine or apple juice (optional)
1 tablespoon dried oregano
1 tablespoon dried thyme
½ teaspoon coarsely ground black pepper

1. Heat the oil in a 13–14-inch skillet and sauté the onions, carrots, peppers, and garlic for 10 minutes.
2. Add the zucchini and mushrooms and cook for 5 minutes.
3. Stir in the tomato sauce, wine, oregano, thyme, and black pepper. Simmer, uncovered, for 20–25 minutes. Serve immediately over hot pasta.

RED BELL PEPPER AND FRESH TOMATO SAUCE

PREPARATION TIME: 15 MINUTES   COOKING TIME: 30 MINUTES   YIELD: 2 QUARTS

2 tablespoons olive oil
6 cups sliced red bell peppers
6 cups roughly chopped fresh tomatoes
1 tablespoon dried basil or oregano
2 garlic cloves, crushed or minced
½ teaspoon coarsely ground black pepper

This sauce is excellent with Spaetzle (page 43), rice, chicken, pork, or ham; however, it doesn't work when made with green bell peppers. Chopped chives or scallion greens (about ½ cup) make a nice addition.

1. Heat the oil in a large skillet and sauté the peppers for 5 minutes. Cover the skillet and cook the peppers for 5 more minutes.
2. Add the tomatoes, basil, garlic, and pepper and cook covered for 20 minutes.
3. Purée in a blender, food processor, or food mill. Then serve over hot pasta.

ANCHOVY SAUCE

PREPARATION TIME: 5 MINUTES   COOKING TIME: 25 MINUTES   YIELD: 3½ CUPS

2 tablespoons olive oil

4–6 garlic cloves, crushed or minced

1 green bell pepper, chopped fine

2 tablespoons chopped parsley

2 tablespoons chopped fresh basil, or
   1 teaspoon dried basil

2 2-ounce cans anchovy filets

½ teaspoon coarsely ground black pepper

3 cups tomato sauce

If you like anchovies, try this sauce. It's great with linguini. Soak the anchovies in cold water first to remove some of the salt, if you wish.

1. Heat the oil in a skillet and sauté the garlic, green pepper, parsley, and basil for 5 minutes.
2. Drain the anchovies and mash them. Add the anchovies to the skillet along with the pepper and tomato sauce. Simmer for 20 minutes. Serve over hot pasta.

CARBONARA SAUCE

2 tablespoons olive oil
2 tablespoons butter
1 garlic clove, crushed or minced
1 shallot, finely chopped
⅓ cup white wine
¼ pound baked or smoked ham, diced small
2 large eggs
½ cup heavy cream
½ cup grated Parmesan cheese
¼ cup chopped parsley or fresh oregano
¼ teaspoon coarsely ground black pepper

1. Heat the oil and the butter in a skillet over medium heat. Add the garlic and shallot and sauté for 1 minute.
2. Add the white wine and heat on high for 2 minutes. Lower the heat, add the ham, and sauté for 1 minute.
3. Beat the eggs and heavy cream together. Stir in the Parmesan, parsley, and pepper.
4. Mix the hot ham with the egg and cream mixture and toss immediately with hot pasta. Serve.

SAUSAGE RAGOUT SAUCE

PREPARATION TIME: 15 MINUTES   COOKING TIME: 45 MINUTES   YIELD: 2 QUARTS

½ pound pork sausage meat or ground pork
2 tablespoons olive oil
1 large onion, chopped
2 medium-size carrots, chopped
4 garlic cloves, crushed or minced
1 large sweet bell pepper, chopped
2 medium-size zucchini, chopped
3 cups fresh tomato sauce, or 1 28-ounce can
   crushed tomatoes
½ cup chopped parsley
2 teaspoons dried thyme
2 teaspoons dried oregano
½ teaspoon coarsely ground black pepper

I prefer either red or yellow bell peppers in this sauce, for their sweetness of flavor. Try this sauce over pasta or as a filling for lasagna.

1. Crumble the sausage meat or pork and brown in a skillet over low heat for 5 minutes. Transfer to a small bowl and drain off the excess fat.
2. Heat the olive oil over medium heat and sauté the onion, carrots, and garlic for 10 minutes.
3. Add the pepper and zucchini and cook for 5 minutes.
4. Return the sausage to the pan along with the tomato sauce and the rest of the ingredients. Stir to combine thoroughly, and simmer on low for 25 minutes. Cover the pan if a thinner ragout is desired. Combine with hot pasta and serve.

JIM STAFFORD'S MUSHROOM-CHEESE SAUCE

PREPARATION TIME: 10 MINUTES   COOKING TIME: 25 MINUTES   YIELD: 4 CUPS

2 tablespoons olive oil

8 ounces mushrooms, sliced

2 garlic cloves, crushed or minced

½ teaspoon coarsely ground black pepper

2 large tomatoes, scalded to remove skins,
    and sliced

2 tablespoons sweet butter or olive oil

2 ounces bleu cheese

2 ounces Swiss cheese

4 ounces mixed odds and ends (goat, mozzarella,
    smoked Gouda, mushroom cheese, etc....)

½ cup tomato sauce with ½ teaspoon sugar,
    or canned spaghetti sauce

This is the invention of a college-student friend of mine. It not only works (amazing though it may seem when you read the cheese ingredients), but it tastes absolutely sensational!

1. Heat the olive oil in a skillet and sauté the mushrooms and garlic for 5 minutes.
2. Add the pepper and sliced tomatoes. Simmer for 10 minutes.
3. While this mixture is cooking, melt the butter in a 2-quart saucepan and add the cheeses, stirring for about 5 minutes, until they are melted.
4. Stir the mushroom-tomato mixture into the melted cheeses and add the tomato sauce and sugar. Combine well and cook for 5 minutes. Serve over hot pasta.

WALNUT SAUCE I

PREPARATION TIME: 5 MINUTES   COOKING TIME: 10 MINUTES   YIELD: 2 CUPS

2 tablespoons olive oil
1 cup chopped walnuts
½ teaspoon coarsely ground black pepper
⅔ cup tomato sauce
½ cup butter

This sauce is wonderful served over linguini and topped with Parmesan cheese.

1. Heat the oil in a skillet and sauté the walnuts for 2 minutes, stirring constantly.
2. Add the pepper, tomato sauce, and butter. Cook over gentle heat for 10 minutes. Serve immediately over hot pasta.

WALNUT SAUCE II

PREPARATION TIME: 5 MINUTES   COOKING TIME: 15 MINUTES   YIELD: 4 CUPS

¼ cup olive oil
1½ cups finely chopped walnuts
2 garlic cloves, crushed or minced
2 cups canned crushed tomatoes
½ cup cream
½ teaspoon coarsely ground black pepper
¼ cup chopped parsley
¼ cup chopped fresh oregano or basil, or
   1 tablespoon dried oregano or basil

Try this one with fettuccine. Don't forget the Parmesan!

1. Heat the oil in a skillet and sauté the walnuts for 3 minutes, stirring constantly.
2. Add the garlic and sauté for 1 minute.
3. Stir in the tomatoes, cream, pepper, parsley, and oregano. Cook uncovered for 10 minutes. Serve immediately over hot pasta.

NO-COOK
SAUCES AND
DRESSINGS

These sauces appear frequently on my table for two good reasons. Because there's no cooking to diminish either the nutrients or the flavor, they are healthful and deliciously tasty. And they can be made in 5 or 10 minutes — while the pasta cooks.

The butter sauces, mayonnaises, and oil dressings can be regarded as vehicles for binding almost any flavoring to hot or cold pasta. However, butter sauces go best with hot pasta. These recipes can be made from few ingredients. They do not provide substantial nutrition, so they are intended for pasta destined to accompany a meat, poultry, or fish dish or for pasta with beans, meat, seafood, or vegetables. It takes no time at all to "put up" a few of these sauces and dressings at one time, and then you can store them in the refrigerator or freezer so they're ready for impromptu meals and lazy or busy days.

NO-COOK HERB SEASONING

PREPARATION TIME: 10 MINUTES   YIELD: 1 CUP

½ cup grated **Parmesan** cheese
¼ cup grated **Romano** cheese
½ cup chopped fresh herbs (parsley,
   basil, oregano)
2 garlic cloves, crushed or minced
½ teaspoon coarsely ground black pepper

*Since this isn't actually a sauce, mix 3–4 table-
spoons of olive oil with a pound of pasta before adding
this excellent seasoning.*

1. Combine the cheeses, herbs, garlic, and
   pepper in a bowl.
2. Serve with hot or cold pasta.

JIFFY HERB AND CHEESE SAUCE

PREPARATION TIME: 5 MINUTES   YIELD: 2¾ CUPS

1 cup parsley
¼ cup fresh basil leaves, or 2 tablespoons dried
   basil
2 garlic cloves
½ teaspoon coarsely ground black pepper
¼ cup olive oil
½ cup low-fat cottage or ricotta cheese
½ cup grated Parmesan cheese
½ cup grated Romano cheese
½ cup cream or half-and-half

1. Remove the stems from the parsley and place
   the parsley in a food processor or blender with
   the basil, garlic, pepper, and olive oil, and
   purée.
2. Add the cheeses and cream. Blend until
   combined. Serve immediately over hot pasta.

BASIL PESTO

PREPARATION TIME: 10 MINUTES   YIELD: 3 CUPS

3 cups basil leaves
3 large garlic cloves
¼ cup vegetable oil
¼ cup olive oil
½ cup tomato juice or carrot juice
¼ cup chopped walnuts
⅓ cup grated Parmesan cheese
⅓ cup grated Romano cheese

As much as I love to eat basil pesto on pasta, I also use it as a spread for garlic bread, and for lamb and pork roasts before they go in the oven. I sometimes stir a tablespoon into soups or the batter for homemade breads and savory muffins. It also goes on fish, mushrooms, and tomatoes that are going under the broiler. It adds zip to many dishes that need something extra. Pesto can be stored for one month in the refrigerator, or up to a year in the freezer.

1. Using a food processor or blender, grind the basil leaves, garlic, oils, and juice together (1 minute if using a food processor).
2. Add the chopped walnuts and blend or process until fine (10 seconds in a processor).
3. Add the cheeses and blend well. Serve.

BASIC SEASONED BUTTER

PREPARATION TIME: 5 MINUTES   YIELD: ¾ CUP

1 stick unsalted butter, softened
2 tablespoons olive oil
1 small garlic clove, crushed
⅛ teaspoon ground white pepper
¼ cup chopped chives

1. Combine all the ingredients in a bowl and mash together until smooth.

2. Chill for half an hour before serving.

Variations

Add one or two of the following ingredients along with or in place of the chives:

- ½ cup chopped parsley
- ½ cup chopped fresh mixed herbs
- 2 tablespoons dried herbs
- 2 tablespoons chopped shallots
- 2 tablespoons fresh lemon juice
- ¼ cup chopped scallions
- ¼ cup crumbled bleu cheese (1 ounce)
- 1 whole anchovy, mashed, or 1½ teaspoons anchovy paste
- 2 tablespoons chopped fresh tarragon
- 2 tablespoons snipped fresh dill
- ½ teaspoon ground ginger, 1 tablespoon sesame paste, and 2 tablespoons chopped chives
- ¼ cup finely ground nuts

BASIC MAYONNAISE

PREPARATION TIME: 5 MINUTES   YIELD: 1–1¼ CUPS

1 large egg
3 tablespoons fresh lemon juice
¼ cup olive oil
1 garlic clove, crushed
1 teaspoon powdered mustard
¾ cup vegetable oil

1. Place the egg, lemon juice, olive oil, garlic, and mustard in a blender and mix on high speed.
2. With the blender on low, slowly add the ¾ cup vegetable oil in one continuous thin stream to thicken the mayonnaise. This will take about 1 minute. When the mayonnaise has thickened, it can be served immediately over cold or hot pasta. Or store it in a well-sealed container in the refrigerator for up to one month.

Variations

Add one or two of the following ingredients:

- 1 tablespoon honey and 2 teaspoons curry powder
- ¼ cup chopped chives or scallions
- 4 garlic cloves, crushed
- 2 tablespoons chopped fresh oregano and 2 tablespoons chopped fresh thyme
- ½ cup puréed red bell pepper
- ¼ cup crumbled bleu cheese (1 ounce)
- 2 tablespoons sesame paste or peanut butter, 1 teaspoon ground ginger, and 1 tablespoon soy sauce
- ¼ cup sour cream or plain yogurt
- ¼ cup puréed watercress

- ¼–½ cup chopped parsley
- ¼ cup puréed fresh basil leaves
- 1 tablespoon dried herbs
- ¼ cup vegetable taco sauce and ½ teaspoon cumin powder

- 1 whole mashed avocado and 1 skinned, chopped tomato
- 2 tablespoons chopped capers
- ¼ cup tomato sauce and 1 teaspoon dried basil, or 6 leaves of fresh basil

COTTAGE-CHEESE-AND-CHIVE TOMATO SAUCE

PREPARATION TIME: 10 MINUTES   YIELD: 3 CUPS

1 cup cottage cheese
1 cup tomato sauce
¼ cup cream (optional)
2 tablespoons olive oil
½ cup grated Parmesan cheese
½ cup finely snipped fresh chives or scallion
   greens
½ teaspoon nutmeg
⅛ teaspoon finely ground black pepper
2 garlic cloves, crushed or minced

1. In a medium-size bowl or a food processor, thoroughly combine all the ingredients.
2. Serve over hot pasta.

BASIC OIL DRESSING

⅓ cup olive oil
1 cup vegetable oil
¼ cup vinegar or fresh lemon juice
1 tablespoon mild prepared mustard
2 garlic cloves, crushed
1 tablespoon dried herbs

This quantity will be adequate for ½ pound of hot pasta or 1 pound cold pasta. (When the pasta is hot, it absorbs some of the dressing.)

1. Place all the ingredients in a large jar with a tight lid and shake to blend.
2. Serve immediately over hot or cold pasta, or store in the refrigerator.

Variations

Add one or two of the following:

- ¼ cup mayonnaise, plain yogurt, or sour cream
- 1 teaspoon curry powder
- 2 tablespoons peanut butter and 1 tablespoon soy sauce
- ¼ cup bleu cheese (1 ounce)
- ¼ cup grated Parmesan or Romano cheese
- 1 teaspoon paprika and 2 tablespoons grated Parmesan cheese
- 2 tablespoons chopped shallots, chives, or scallions
- ¼ cup finely chopped walnuts
- ½ cup cooked and mashed garbanzo beans (chickpeas)
- ½ cup mashed avocado

SEAFOOD BUTTER

6 medium-size shrimp, shelled, cooked 2
    minutes in boiling water, and puréed
1 stick unsalted butter, softened
¼ teaspoon paprika
⅛ teaspoon ground white pepper
1 small garlic clove, crushed (optional)

1. Combine all the ingredients in a bowl and mash together until smooth.
2. Chill for half an hour before serving.

Variations

In place of the shrimp try:

- ½ 7-ounce can tuna, mashed
- 1 whole anchovy, mashed, or 1½ teaspoons anchovy paste
- ¼ cup finely chopped smoked salmon with ¼ cup chopped parsley, if desired

QUANTITY PASTA RECIPES

The three recipes in this chapter come from Dick Rossi, food consultant to the New York Giants, who has been helping those athletes change their eating habits over the past couple of years. These are recipes that he prepared for the Giants Training Camp. Rossi recommends using low-fat cheeses, fresh vegetables, and polyunsaturated oils (such as safflower, sunflower, or corn oil) whenever possible. Anyone who wants to improve his or her diet can benefit from these recipes, which are based on the same principles of good health as the other recipes in this book.

These recipes are offered for more than human interest. If you have an occasion to cook for a *large* number of people, try one of these recipes. For family-sized dishes, divide the 100-serving recipes by four and use two regular lasagna pans. Freeze one pan, if you like, before or after baking.

DICK ROSSI'S CAPONATA SPAGHETTI

PREPARATION TIME: 60 MINUTES   COOKING TIME: 60 MINUTES   YIELD: 25–30 SERVINGS

4½ cups vegetable oil
4 pounds large onions, chopped
2¼ tablespoons garlic powder
2¼ pounds green bell peppers, chopped
3⅔ pounds mushrooms, sliced
4 pounds eggplant, peeled and cubed
3 quarts plain commercial spaghetti sauce
3⅓ cups water
2 cups wine vinegar
4 tablespoons dried oregano
¼ cup granulated sugar
2½ tablespoons salt
1½ tablespoons coarsely ground black pepper
6¾ pounds thin spaghetti
3 gallons water
7 tablespoons salt
3⅓ tablespoons vegetable oil

1. Heat the oil in a large stockpot and add the onions and garlic powder. Sauté gently for 15 minutes.
2. Add the peppers, mushrooms, and eggplant. Cook on low for 10 minutes, stirring occasionally.
3. Add the next seven ingredients. Mix thoroughly and simmer, covered, until the eggplant is tender, about 20 minutes. Stir frequently.
4. Cook the spaghetti in 3 gallons of water with the salt and vegetable oil for 5 minutes. Drain and rinse. Reheat in hot (but not boiling) water just before serving. Drain again and top each portion with about ½ cup of sauce.

DICK ROSSI'S LASAGNA

PREPARATION TIME: 60 MINUTES   COOKING TIME: 40 MINUTES   SETTING TIME: 20 MINUTES
YIELD: 100 SERVINGS

3¼ tablespoons vegetable oil

1⅔ tablespoons chopped garlic

1⅔ teaspoons dried oregano

1⅔ teaspoons dried basil

¼ teaspoon ground black pepper

3¼ cups water

10½ pounds plain commercial spaghetti
    sauce (1⅓ gallons)

¾ cup red wine

15 pounds part-skim ricotta cheese (30 cups)

15 pounds part-skim mozzarella, shredded
    (60 cups)

5 pounds Parmesan cheese, grated (20 cups)

10 whole fresh eggs, beaten, or 3 cups
    cholesterol-free egg substitute

2½ tablespoons dried oregano

¼ teaspoon ground black pepper

10½ pounds lasagna noodles, cooked according
    to package directions

6 pounds part-skim mozzarella, shredded
    (22 cups)

8 ounces Parmesan cheese, grated (2 cups)

*You will need four extra-large lasagna pans
(12x18x4) for this recipe.*

1. Heat the oil and sauté the garlic, the 1⅔ teaspoons oregano, the 1⅔ teaspoons basil, and the ¼ teaspoon pepper for 1 minute. Do not brown.
2. Add the water, spaghetti sauce, and red wine and simmer for 30 minutes.
3. Mix the ricotta, the 15 pounds mozzarella, the 5 pounds Parmesan, the eggs, 2½ tablespoons oregano, and ¼ teaspoon pepper. Divide this mixture into four equal portions (for the four pans) and set aside.
4. Preheat the oven to 350° F.
5. Spread 1 cup of sauce on the bottom of each pan, and place a layer of lasagna noodles on top.
6. Spread one-third of a portion of the ricotta mixture on top of the noodles in each pan. Sprinkle with 1½ cups of shredded mozzarella, and 2 tablespoons of grated Parmesan.
7. Repeat the layers two more times, using up all of the ricotta mixture.
8. Cover the top layer of cheeses with another layer of noodles, spread the noodles with 2 cups of sauce, 1½ cups of mozzarella cheese, and 2 tablespoons of grated Parmesan.

9. Bake covered for 30 minutes. Uncover and bake for 10 more minutes. Allow 20 minutes for this dish to set before cutting and serving.

DICK ROSSI'S BAKED ZITI

PREPARATION TIME: 30 MINUTES   COOKING TIME: 1 HOUR, 15 MINUTES   YIELD: 100 SERVINGS

3 gallons water
6¼ pounds macaroni ziti
3⅔ tablespoons vegetable oil
1⅔ tablespoons salt
19⅓ pounds plain commercial spaghetti sauce
   (2⅓ gallons)
10 whole fresh eggs, beaten, or 3 cups
   cholesterol-free egg substitute
6 pounds low-fat cottage cheese (12 cups)
6¼ pounds part-skim mozzarella cheese,
   shredded (25 cups)
1⅔ pounds Parmesan cheese, grated (7 cups)

Use three extra-large lasagna pans (12x18x4) for this recipe.

1. Bring the water to a boil and cook the ziti with the oil and salt for 10 minutes. Drain.
2. Preheat the oven to 350° F.
3. Mix the spaghetti sauce with the pasta and divide this mixture into three equal portions (for the three pans).
4. Combine the eggs and cottage cheese.
5. Combine the mozzarella and Parmesan cheeses.
6. Spread one-third of a portion of the pasta-sauce mixture in the bottom of each pan.
7. Top with 2½ cups of the egg mixture and 4⅓ cups of the cheese mixture.
8. Repeat all the layers once. Then make a third layer of the pasta-sauce mixture and top it with 2 cups of the cheese mixture.
9. Bake for 1 hour and 15 minutes. Each pan should yield approximately 32 servings.

Index

Anchovy paste, seafood butter, 143
Anchovy sauce, 130
Ann Kojis's
  cold spicy Szechuan noodles, 93
  quick lasagna, 49
  spaetzle, 43
Ann Nappi's macaroni with meat and sauce, 67
Asparagus, carrot and, spaghetti, 116
Athletics, 8-11
Avocado sauce, shells with, 103

Baked macaroni ricotta, 53
Baked ziti, Dick Rossi's, 149
Basic mayonnaise, 140-41
Basic oil dressing, 142
Basic pasta recipe, 25-27
Basic seasoned butter, 139
Basil pesto, 138
Basil, and tomato pasta salad, mozzarella, 103
Bean(s). *See also* Legumes
  lamb, and ditalini soup, 57
  Mexican, and macaroni, 109
  and pasta with fresh tomato sauce, 59
  salad, macaroni and three-, 109
  soup, vegetable, tubettini, and, 62
  white kidney, and scallions, 107
Beef
  Ann Nappi's macaroni with meat and sauce, 67
  ginger noodles with flank steak, 99
  pot roast with egg noodles, 68
  sausage meatballs with ziti, 71
  traditional lasagna, 48-49
Broccoli, shells, mushroom-, 117
Broccoli twist, 118
Buckwheat noodles, 18
Butter
  basic seasoned, 139
  seafood, 143

Cacciatore, chicken livers hunter style, 75
Cannelloni, 26
  Mona Trattoria's, 38-39
Caponata spaghetti, Dick Rossi's, 147
Carbohydrates, 10
  complex, 5-7, 10-11
  simple, 5
Carbonara sauce, 131
Carol Harcarik's pasta dough, 32
Carol Harcarik's pasta primavera salad, 110
Carrot and asparagus spaghetti, 116
Casserole, Giorgios' Sicilian venison, 70
Cavatelli primavera, 120
Cheese
  baked macaroni ricotta, 53
  Mona Trattoria's gnocchi di ricotta, 40-41
  mozzarella
    basil, and tomato pasta salad, 103
    and fusilli, zucchini, 115
    with sweet red peppers, prosciutto-, 121
  pasta, 28
  ravioli, spinach and, 42-43
  sauce
    jiffy herb and, 137
    Jim Stafford's mushroom-, 133
    Parmesan cream, 37
Chicken
  curry macaroni, 108
  -garbanzo soup, 58
  livers hunter style, 75
  marinated, with sesame noodles, 98
  -spinach lasagna, 51
  stir fry with noodles, 94
  stock, 62
  white meat ravioli, 41
Chinese noodles, 18. *See also* Oriental noodles; Noodles
  Ann Kojis's cold spicy Szechuan noodles, 93
  marinated chicken with sesame noodles, 98

Chive tomato sauce, cottage-cheese-and-, 141
Cholesterol, 7-9
Clam sauce
  red, linguini with, 84
  white, with thin spaghetti, 85
Cod, 78
Cooking pasta, 16-19
  yield, 16
Cottage-cheese-and-chive tomato sauce, 141
Crab
  alla Alfredo, 86
  dill, and shell salad, 87
Cream sauce, Parmesan, 37
Curried lentils and ditalini, 106
Curried tofu sauce, 126
Curry macaroni, chicken, 108

Dick Rossi's
  baked ziti, 149
  caponata spaghetti, 147
  lasagna, 148-49
Ditalini, curried lentils and, 106
Ditalini, soup, lamb, bean, and, 57
Dressing(s), 136. *See also* Sauce
  basic mayonnaise, 140-41
  basic oil, 142
  basic seasoned butter, 139
  basil pesto, 138
  no-cook herb seasoning, 137
  seafood butter, 143

Easy eggplant lasagna, 50
Egg noodles. *See also* Noodles; Oriental noodles
  pot roast with, 68
  varieties, 17-18
  wheat, 18
Egg rolls, tofu, 95
Egg wheat noodles, 18
Eggless pasta, 28

Eggplant lasagna, easy, 50

Farmhouse soup, 61
Fat, 8-11
Fettuccine, smoked salmon with, 90
Fettuccine shrimp jambalaya, 80
Flank steak, ginger noodles with, 99
Fried won tons with spicy sauce, 96
Frittata, tomato-spinach pasta, 119
Fusilli
    and piquant tomato sauce, tenderloin of
        pork with, 69
    and sauce, 69
    zucchini, mozzarella, and, 115

Garbanzo soup, chicken-, 58
Garbanzo, pasta pilaf, 60
Garlic-and-mushroom pasta, simple, 122
Ginger noodles with flank steak, 99
Giorgios' Sicilian venison casserole, 70
Giorgios' venison and mushroom sauce over
    vermicelli, 74
Gnocchi di ricotta, Mona Trattoria's, 40-41

Herb and cheese sauce, jiffy, 137
Herb seasoning, no-cook, 137
Homemade pasta, 21-44
    basic pasta recipe, 25-27
    Carol Harcarik's pasta dough, 32
    cheese pasta, 28
    eggless pasta, 28
    nut pasta, 29
    pasta all'uovo, 31
    pasta verde, 29
    shrimp, 30
    storing, 22

Jambalaya, fettuccine shrimp, 80
Japanese noodles, 18. See also Oriental
    noodles; Noodles
Jiffy herb and cheese sauce, 137
Jim Brady's orzo salad, 104
Jim Stafford's mushroom-cheese sauce, 133

Kidney beans, white, and scallions, 107
Kreplach, 44

Lamb, bean, and ditalini soup, 57
Lasagna
    Ann Kojis's quick, 49
    chicken-spinach, 51
    Dick Rossi's, 148-49
    easy eggplant, 50
    traditional, 48-49
Legumes, 56
    beans and pasta with fresh tomato sauce,
        59
    chicken-garbanzo soup, 58
    curried lentils and ditalini, 106
    farmhouse soup, 61
    lamb, bean, and ditalini soup, 57
    macaroni and three-bean salad, 109
    Mexican beans and macaroni, 63
    pasta pilaf garbanzo, 60
    vegetable, tubettini, and bean soup, 62
    white kidney beans and scallions, 107
Lentils
    curried, and ditalini, 106
    farmhouse soup, 61
Linguini
    with red clam sauce, 84
    shrimp and scallops with, 82
    steamed mussels with, 88
Low-fat diet, 8-11

Macaroni, 15
    chicken curry, 108
    description/substitutes, 17
    history, 4-5
    with meat and sauce, Ann Nappi's, 67
    Mexican beans and, 63
    ricotta, baked, 53
    salad, mushroom and, 105
    and three-bean salad, 109
    varieties, 4-5, 15-17
Manicotti, 26, 47
Marinated chicken with sesame noodles, 98
Mayonnaise, basic, 140-41
Meat
    fried won tons with spicy sauce, 96
    ginger noodles with flank steak, 99
    Giorgios' Sicilian venison casserole, 70

Meat (continued)
    Giorgios' venison and mushroom sauce
        over vermicelli, 74
    kreplach, 44
    oxtail soup, 58-59
    pot roast with egg noodles, 68
    ravioli, white meat, 41
    sausage meatballs with ziti, 71
    sausage ragout sauce, 132
    and sauce, Ann Nappi's macaroni with, 67
Meatballs, sausage, with ziti, 71
Mexican beans and macaroni, 63
Mona Trattoria('s), 34
    cannelloni, 38-39
    gnocchi di ricotta, 40-41
    tagliatelle verde al prosciutto, 35
    tortellini with cream sauce, 36-37
Monkfish, 78
Mozzarella
    basil, and tomato pasta salad, 103
    and fusilli, zucchini, 115
    with sweet red peppers, prosciutto-, 121
Mung bean noodles, 18
Mushroom(s)
    -broccoli shells, 117
    -cheese sauce, Jim Stafford's, 133
    and macaroni salad, 105
    pasta, simple garlic-and-, 122
    sauce, 73
        over vermicelli, the Giorgios' venison
            and, 74
        turkey breast with pasta and, 72
    vegetable sauce, 128
    -and-walnut tomato sauce, 127
    and wine, pasta with, 119
Mussels
    rémoulade, 89
    steamed, with linguini, 88

New York Giants, 10-11, 146
No-cook herb seasoning, 137
Noodles, 15. See also Oriental noodles;
    Japanese noodles; Chinese noodles
    Ann Kojis's cold spicy Szechuan, 93
    chicken stir fry with, 94

Noodles *(continued)*
  egg
    pot roast with, 68
    varieties, 17-18
    wheat, 18
  ginger, with flank steak, 99
  history, 3-4
  marinated chicken with sesame, 98
  pot roast with egg, 68
  varieties, 3-4, 15-18
Nut pasta, 29
Nutrition, 4-11, 146
Nutritive Value of Foods, 4

Oil dressing, basic, 142
Olive salad, tuna and, 111
Oriental noodles, 3-4, 15-16, 18. *See also*
  Noodles; Chinese noodles; Japanese
  noodles
  Ann Kojis's cold spicy Szechuan noodles,
    93
  chicken stir fry with noodles, 94
  ginger noodles with flank steak, 99
  marinated chicken with sesame noodles,
    98
Orzo salad, Jim Brady's, 104
Oxtail soup, 58-59

Parmesan cream sauce, 37
Pasta, 3-4, 15
  all'uovo, 31
  beans and, with fresh tomato sauce, 59
  cheese, 28
  cooking, 16-19
  description/substitutes, 17
  dough, Carol Harcarik's, 32
  dry/cooked yield, 16
  eating, 19
  eggless, 28
  fresh, 21-44
  history, 3-4
  machines, 21-22, 26-27
  making, 21-32
  mixing, 26

Pasta *(continued)*
  and mushroom sauce, turkey breast with,
    72-73
  with mushrooms and wine, 119
  nut, 29
  nutritional value, 4-11
  pilaf garbanzo, 60
  recipe, basic, 25-27
  rolling by hand, 26
  serving, 19
  shrimp, 30
  simple garlic-and-mushroom, 122
  soufflé, 52
  stuffed dishes, 34
  varieties, 3-4, 15-17
  verde, 29
  wines, complementary, 19-20
Pasta salad, 102
  Carol Harcarik's pasta primavera salad,
    110
  chicken curry macaroni, 108
  curried lentils and ditalini, 106
  Jim Brady's orzo, 104
  macaroni and three-bean, 109
  mozzarella, basil, and tomato, 103
  mushroom and macaroni, 105
  shells with avocado sauce, 103
  tuna and olive, 111
  white kidney beans and scallions, 107
Pepper(s)
  prosciutto-mozzarella with sweet red, 121
  red bell, and fresh tomato sauce, 129
  vegetable sauce, 128
Pesto, basil, 138
Pilaf garbanzo, pasta, 60
Pork
  fried won tons with spicy sauce, 96
  sausage meatballs with ziti, 71
  tenderloin of, with fusilli and piquant
    tomato sauce, 69
Pot roast with egg noodles, 68
Prosciutto
  -mozzarella with sweet red peppers, 121
  Mona Trattoria's tagliatelle verde al, 35

Protein, 8-10
  complementary, 5-6

Quantity cooking
  Dick Rossi's
    baked ziti, 149
    caponata spaghetti, 147
    lasagna, 148-49

Ragout sauce, sausage, 132
Ravioli, 26
  spinach and cheese, 42-43
  white meat, 41
Red bell pepper and fresh tomato sauce, 129
Rice flour noodles, 18
Ricotta, baked macaroni, 53
Ricotta, Mona Trattoria's gnocchi di, 40-41
Rossi, Dick, 10, 146-49

Salad. *See also* Pasta salad
  crab, dill, and shell, 87
Salmon
  seafood butter, 143
  smoked, with fettuccine, 90
Sauce(s), 124, 136. *See also* Dressing
  anchovy, 130
  avocado, shells with, 103
  carbonara, 131
  cottage-cheese-and-chive tomato, 141
  cream, Mona Trattoria's tortellini with,
    36-37
  curried tofu, 126
  fusilli and, 69
  jiffy herb and cheese, 137
  Jim Stafford's mushroom-cheese, 133
  mushroom, 73
  mushroom-and-walnut tomato, 127
  Parmesan cream, 37
  red bell pepper and fresh tomato, 129
  red clam, linguini with, 84
  sausage ragout, 132
  shrimp, 127
  spicy, 97
  tomato, 71

Sauce(s) *(continued)*
   tomato, I, 125
   tomato, II, 125
   tuna, ziti with, 79
   vegetable, 128
   venison and mushroom, over vermicelli, Giorgios', 74
   walnut, I, 134
   walnut, II, 134
   white clam, with thin spaghetti, 85
   zucchini-tomato, 126
Sausage(s)
   Ann Nappi's macaroni with meat and sauce, 67
   meatballs with ziti, 71
   ragout sauce, 132
   traditional lasagna, 48-49
Scallions, white kidney beans and, 107
Scallops, 78
   seafood and shells, 83
   with linguini, shrimp and, 82
Seafood, 78
   butter, 143
   crab, dill, and shell salad, 87
   crab alla Alfredo, 86
   fettuccine shrimp jambalaya, 80
   linguini with red clam sauce, 84
   monkfish, 78
   mussels rémoulade, 89
   and shells, 83
   shrimp pasta, 30
   shrimp and scallops with linguini, 82
   shrimp sauce, 127
   smoked salmon with fettuccine, 90
   steamed mussels with linguini, 88
   tarragon shrimp with twists, 81
   tuna and olive salad, 111
   white clam sauce with thin spaghetti, 85
   ziti with tuna sauce, 79
Seasoned butter, basic, 139
Seasoning, no-cook herb, 137
Seaweed noodles, 18
Senate Select Committee on Nutrition, 6, 8
Serving pasta, 19

Sesame noodles, marinated chicken with, 98
Sesame paste
   ginger noodles with flank steak, 99
   marinated chicken with sesame noodles, 98
Shell(s)
   with avocado sauce, 103
   mushroom-broccoli, 117
   salad, 87
   seafood and, 83
Shrimp, 78
   jambalaya, fettuccine, 80
   pasta, 30
   sauce, 127
   and scallops with linguini, 82
   seafood and shells, 83
   seafood butter, 143
   with twists, tarragon, 81
Simple garlic-and-mushroom pasta, 122
Smoked salmon with fettuccine, 90
Soufflé, pasta, 52
Soup
   chicken-garbanzo, 58
   farmhouse, 61
   lamb, bean, and ditalini, 57
   oxtail, 58-59
   vegetable, tubettini, and bean, 62
Spaetzle, Ann Kojis's, 43
Spaghetti
   carrot and asparagus, 116
   description/substitutes, 17
   Dick Rossi's caponata, 147
   thin, white clam sauce with, 85
Spicy sauce, 97
   fried won tons with, 96
Spinach
   and cheese ravioli, 42-43
   lasagna, chicken-, 51
   pasta frittata, tomato-, 119
Split peas
   farmhouse soup, 61
Steamed mussels with linguini, 88
Stuffed pasta
   description/substitutes, 17

Stuffed pasta *(continued)*
   dishes, 34
Szechuan noodles, Ann Kojis's cold spicy, 93

Tagliatelle verde al prosciutto, Mona Trattoria's, 35
Tahini. *See* Sesame paste
Tarragon shrimp with twists, 81
Tenderloin of pork with fusilli and piquant tomato sauce, 69
Tofu egg rolls, 95
Tofu sauce, curried, 126
Tomato
   -spinach pasta frittata, 119
   pasta salad, mozzarella, basil, and, 103
   sauce, 71
      I, 125
      II, 125
      beans and pasta with fresh, 59
      cottage-cheese-and-chive, 141
      mushroom-and-walnut, 127
      red bell pepper and fresh, 129
      zucchini-, 126
Tortellini, 26
Tortellini with cream sauce, Mona Trattoria's, 36-37
Traditional lasagna, 48-49
Tubettini, vegetable, and bean soup, 62
Tuna
   and olive salad, 111
   sauce, ziti with, 79
   seafood butter, 143
   white meat ravioli, 41
Turkey breast with pasta and mushroom sauce, 72-73

USDA, 4
   Human Nutrition Center, 6

Veal, white meat ravioli, 41
Vegetable, tubettini, and bean soup, 62
Vegetable dishes
   broccoli twist, 118

Vegetables *(continued)*
  carrot and asparagus spaghetti, 116
  cavatelli primavera, 120
  mushroom-broccoli shells, 117
  pasta with mushrooms and wine, 119
  prosciutto-mozzarella with sweet red
    peppers, 121
  simple garlic-and-mushroom pasta, 122
  tomato-spinach pasta frittata, 119
  vegetable, tubettini, and bean soup, 62
  zucchini, mozzarella, and fusilli, 115
Vegetable sauce, 128
Venison casserole, Giorgios' Sicilian, 70

Venison and mushroom sauce over
  vermicelli, Giorgio's, 74

Walnut
  sauce I, 134
  sauce II, 134
  tomato sauce, mushroom-and-, 127
Wheat flour noodles, 18
White clam sauce with thin spaghetti, 85
White kidney beans and scallions, 107
White meat ravioli, 41
Wine, 19-20
  pasta with mushrooms and, 119

Won tons, fried, with spicy sauce, 96

Yam flour noodles, 18

Ziti
  baked, Dick Rossi's, 149
  sausage meatballs with, 71
  with tuna sauce, 79
Zucchini
  -tomato sauce, 126
  mozzarella, and fusilli, 115
  vegetable sauce, 128